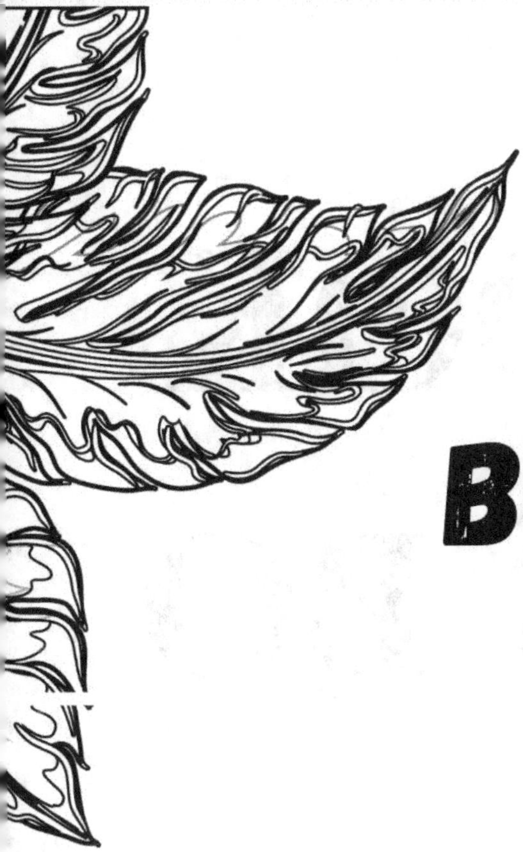

FRUITS COLORING BOOK FOR KIDS AGES 4-8

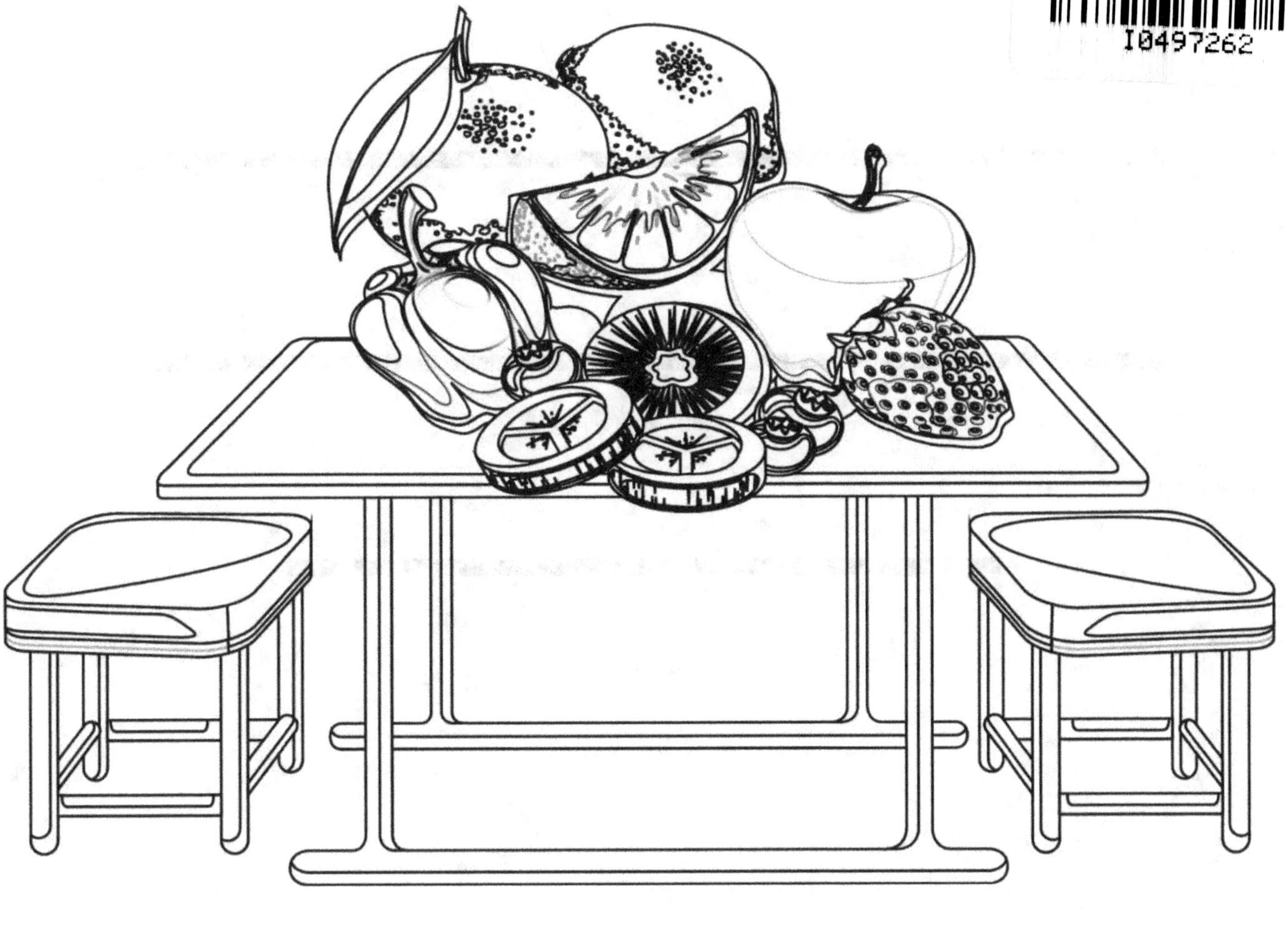

THIS BOOK BELONG BO

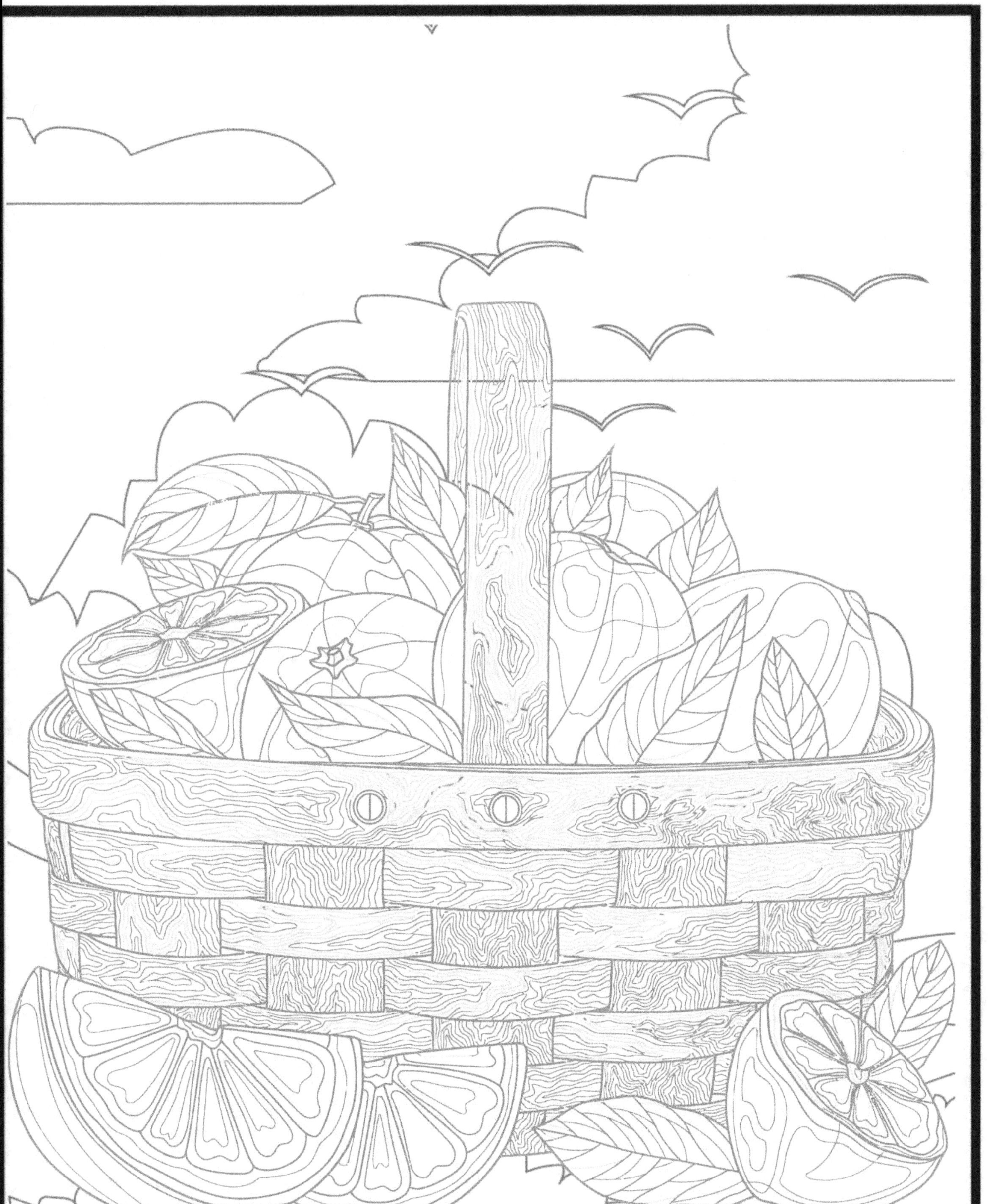

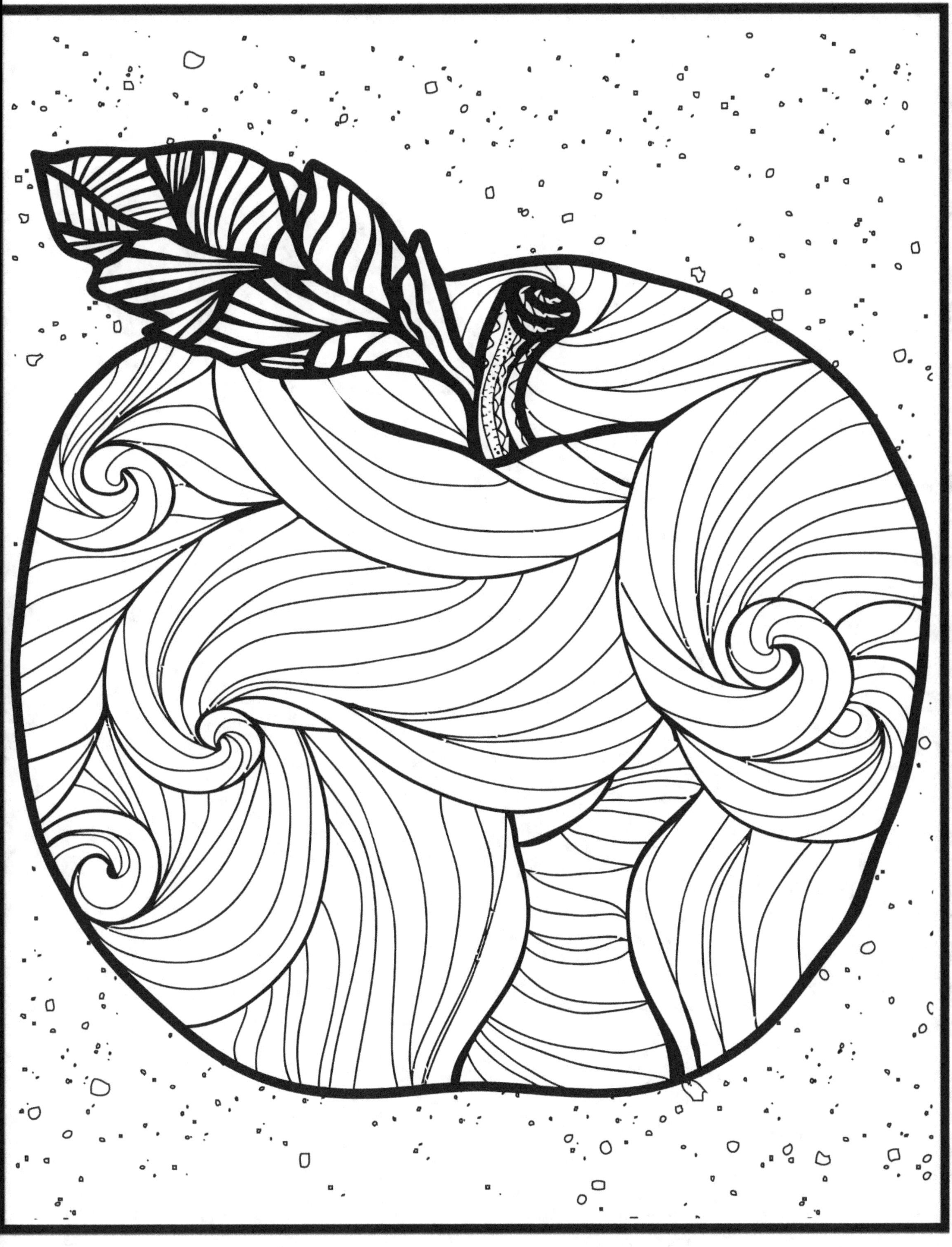

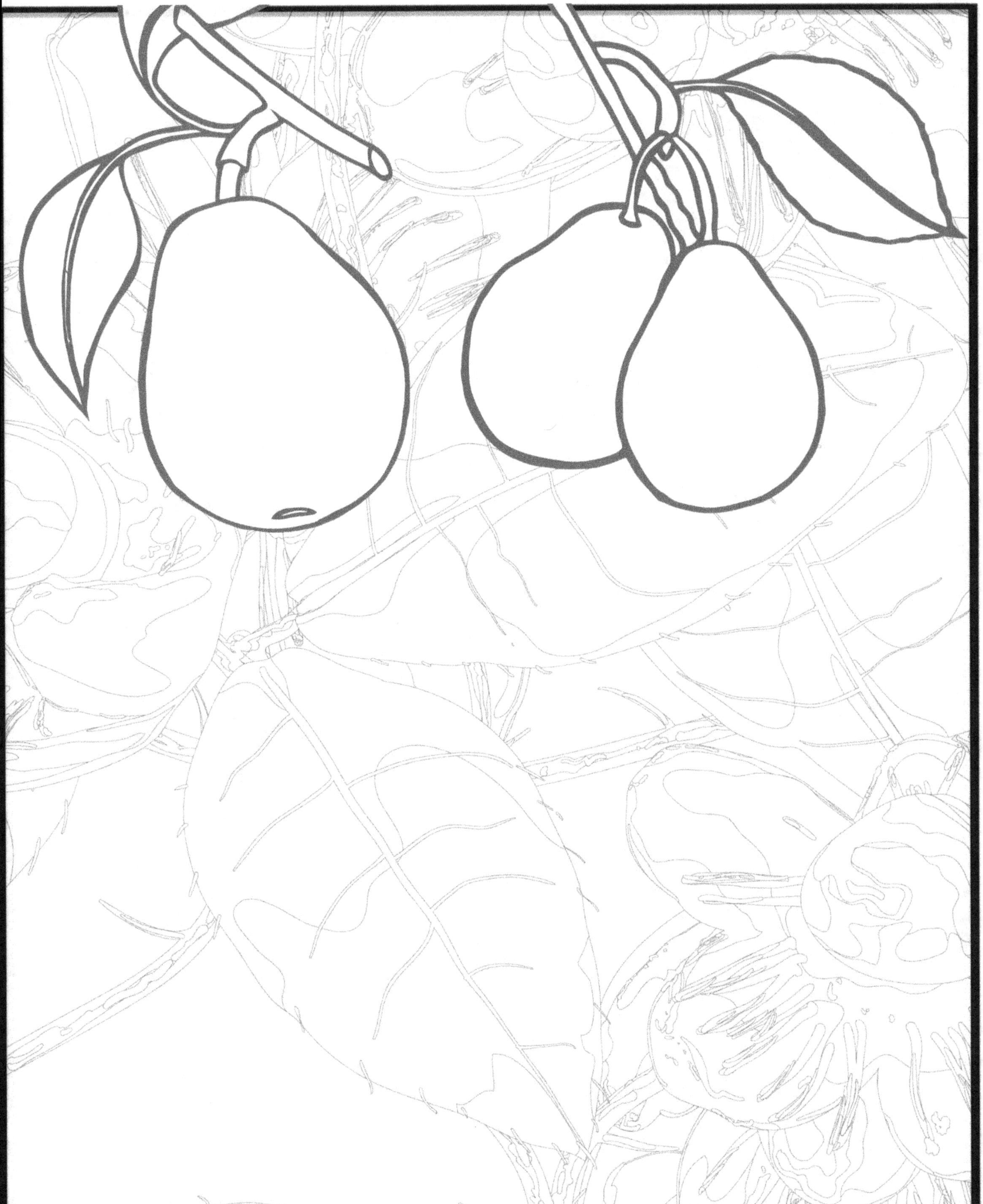

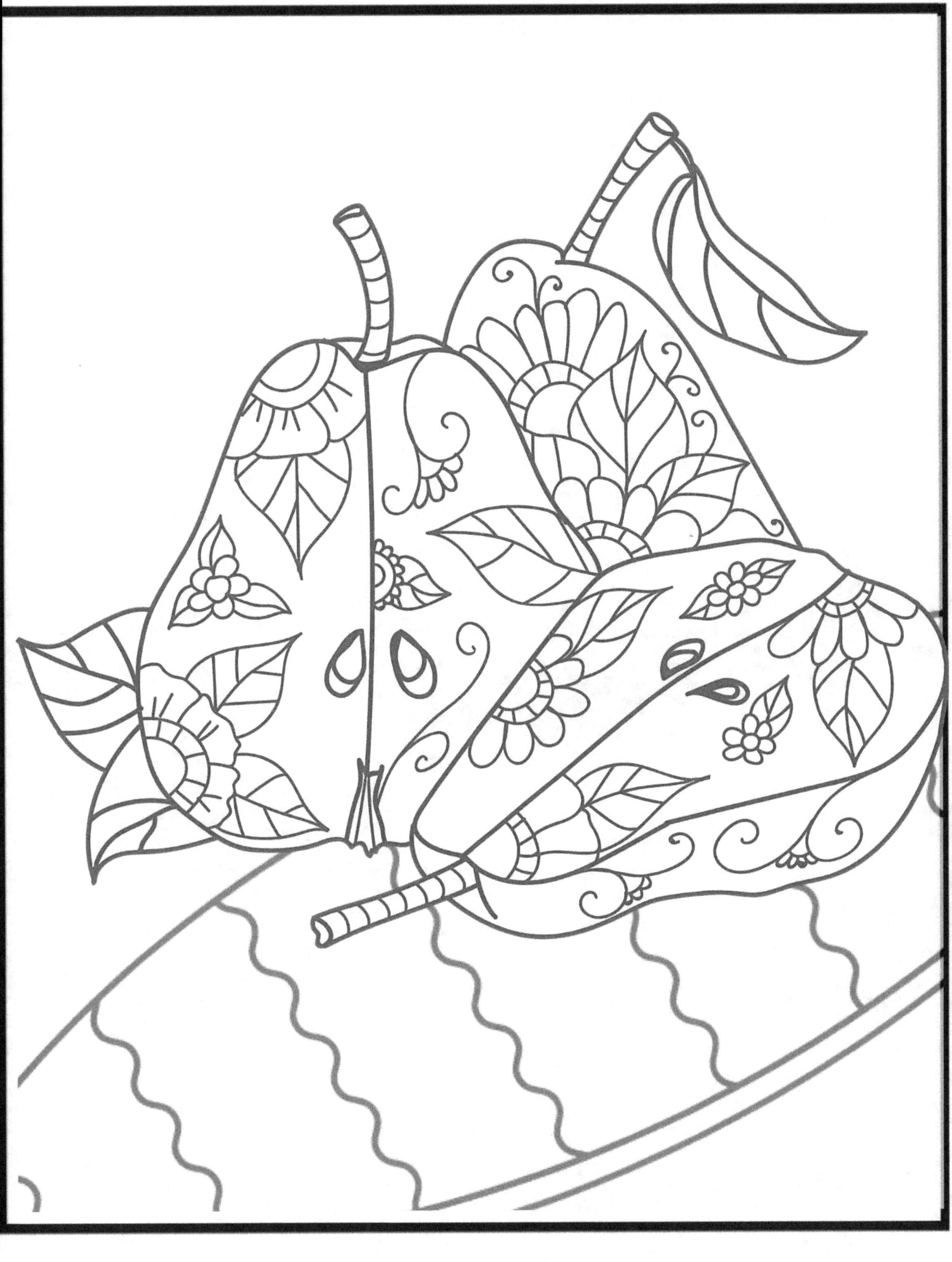

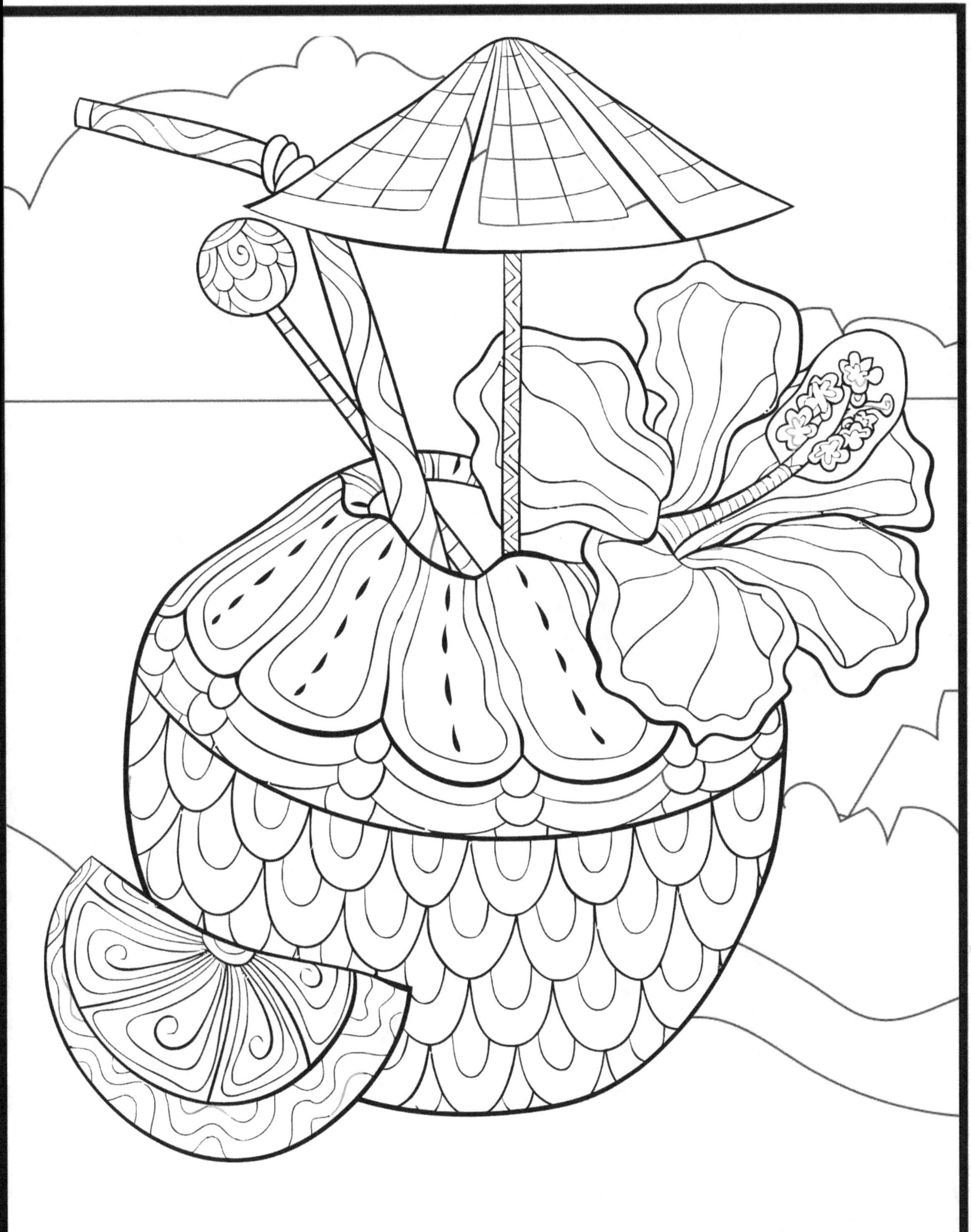

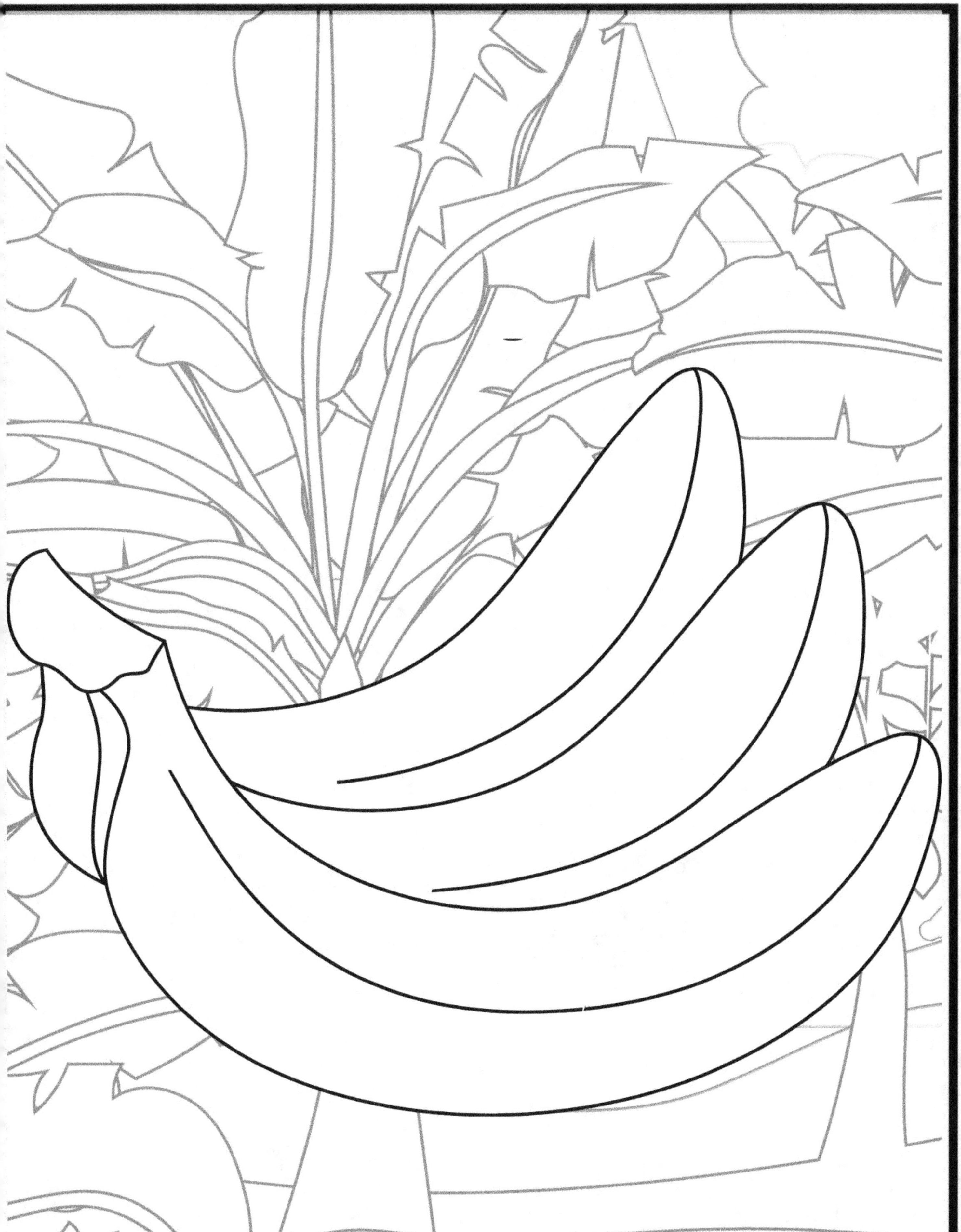

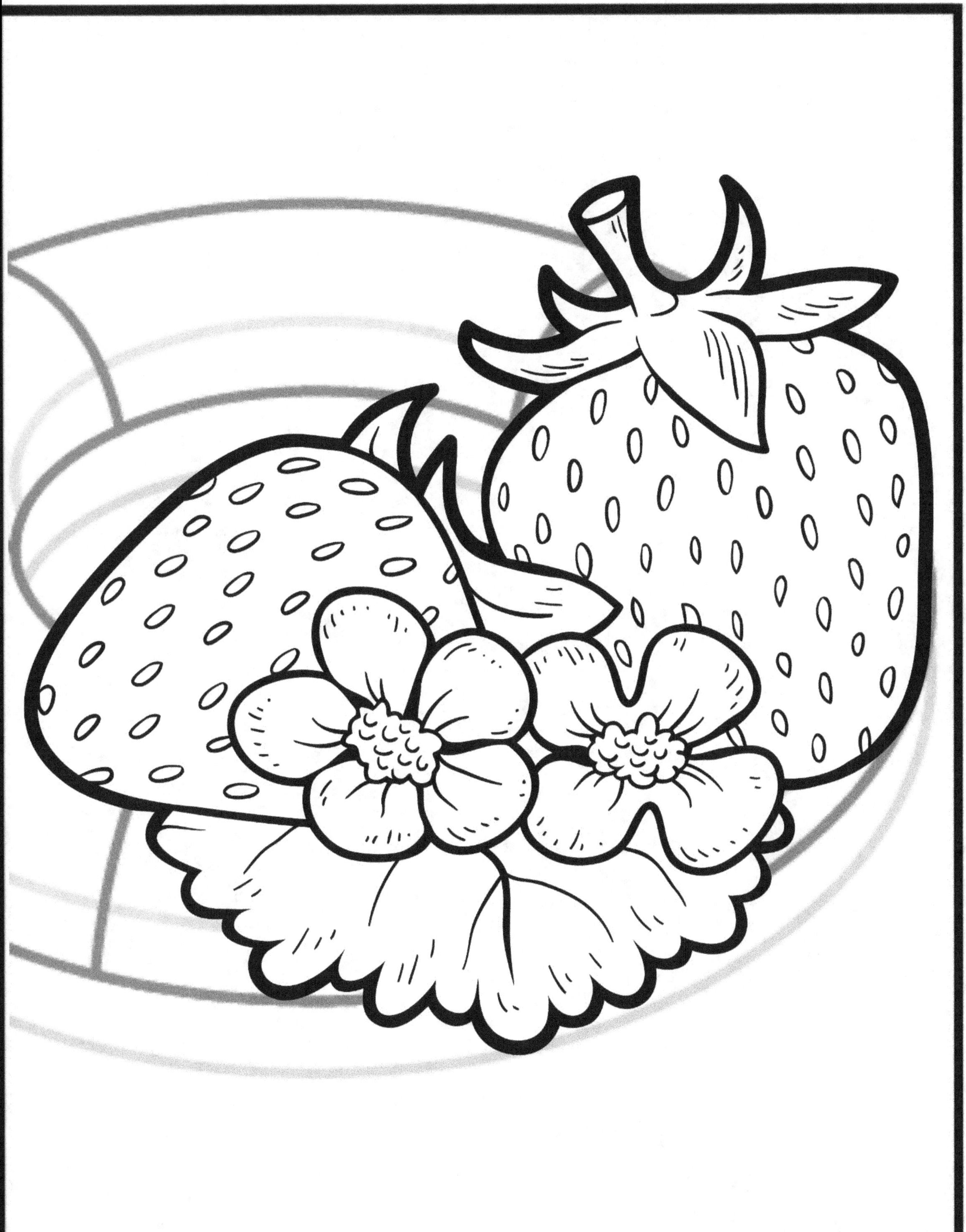

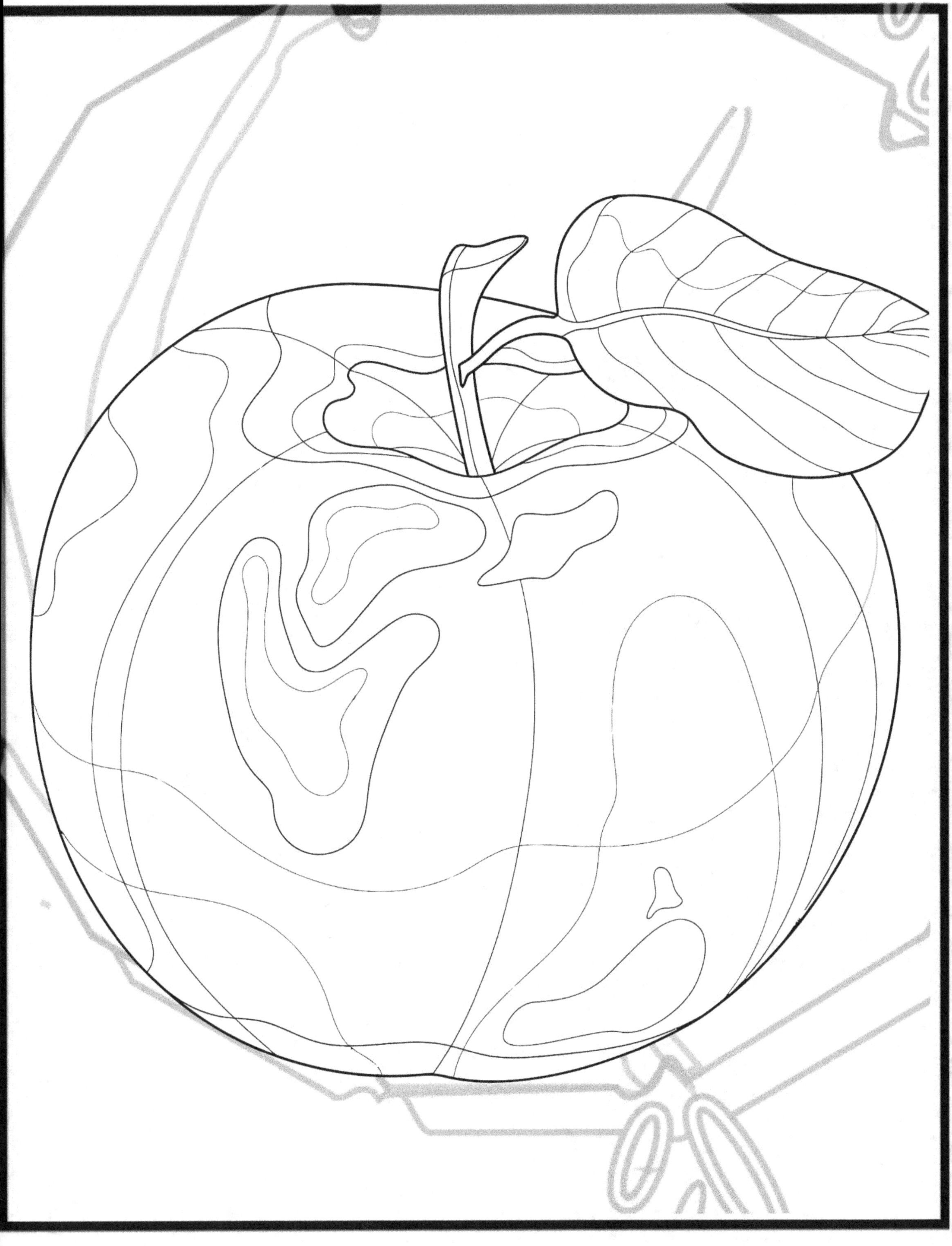

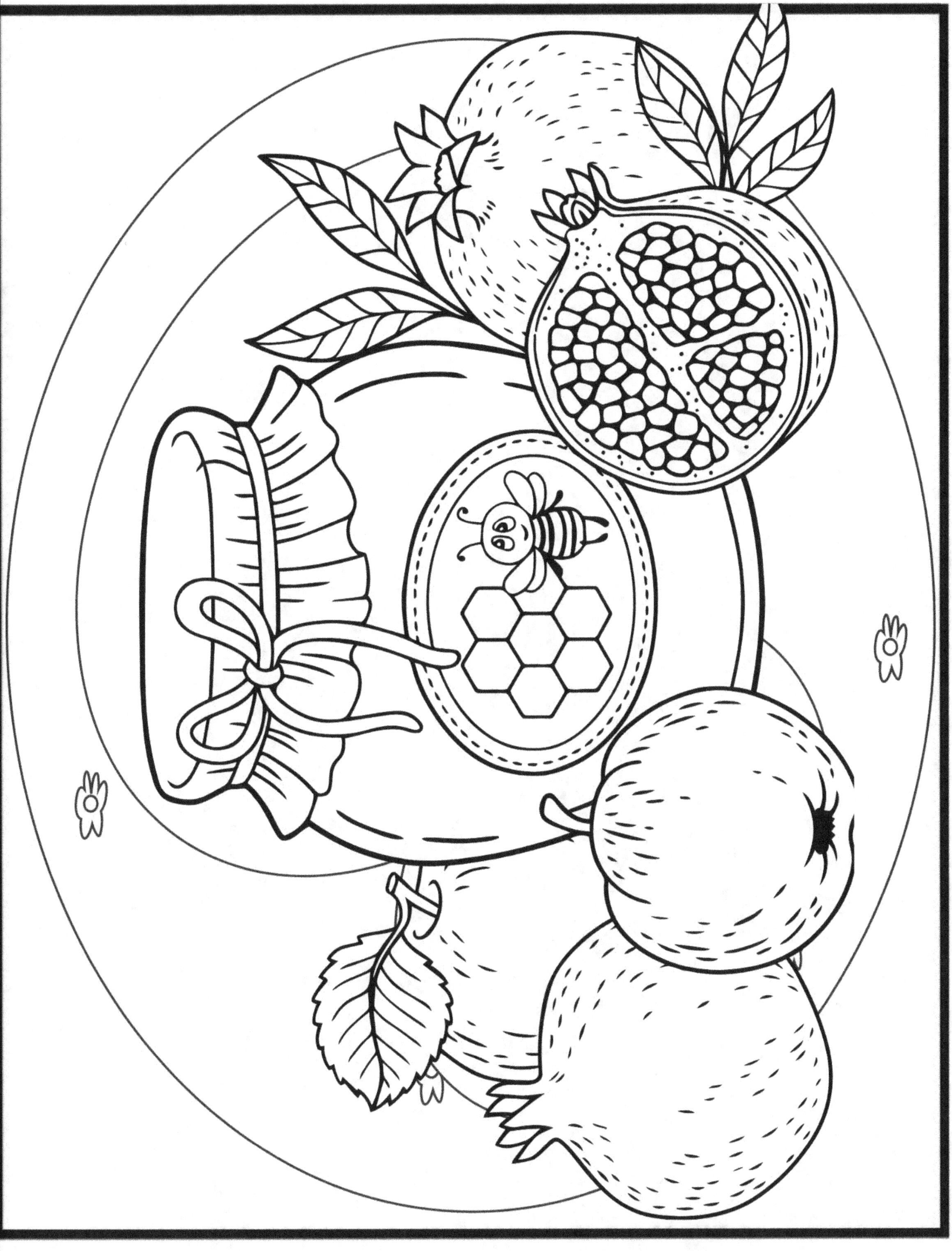

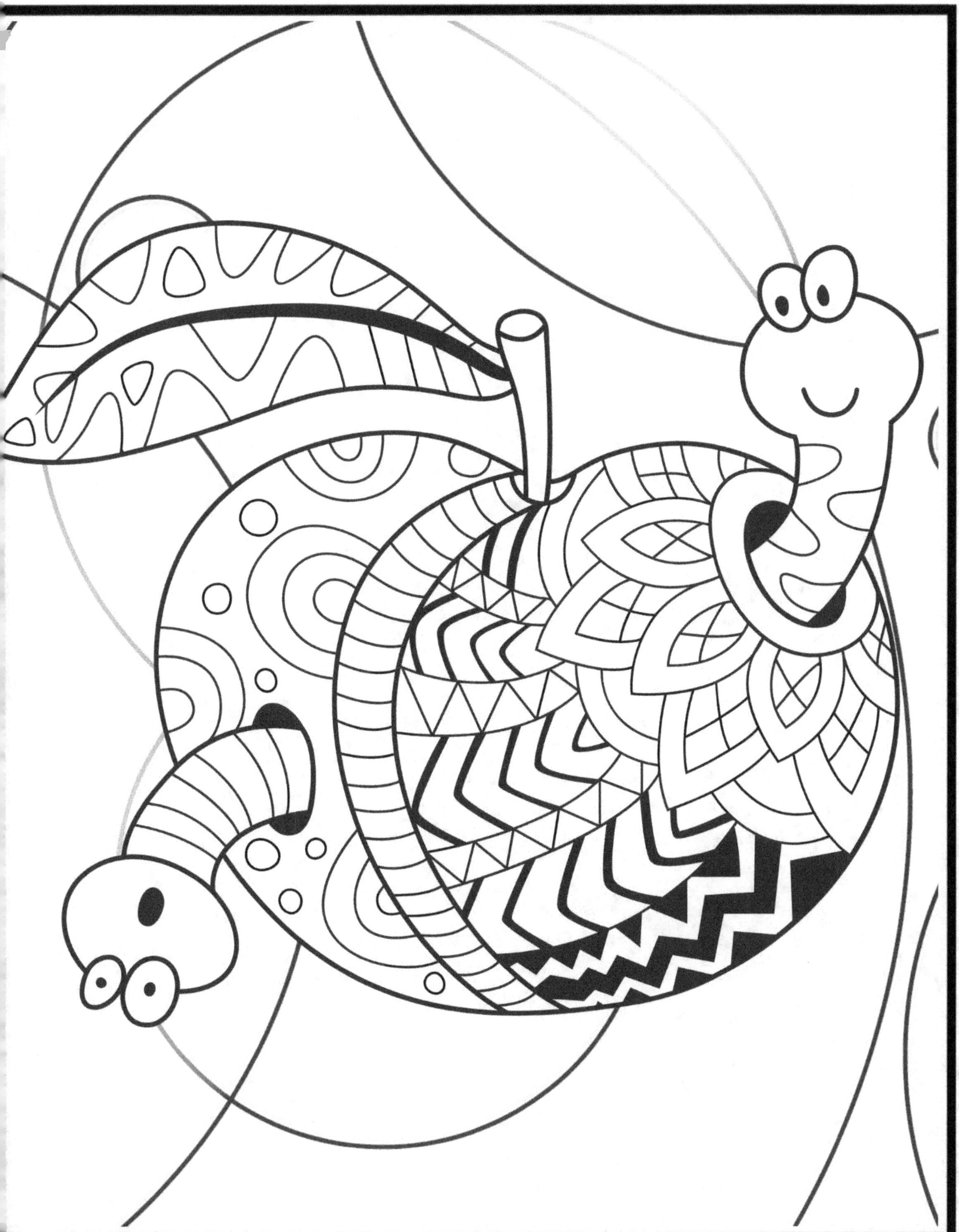

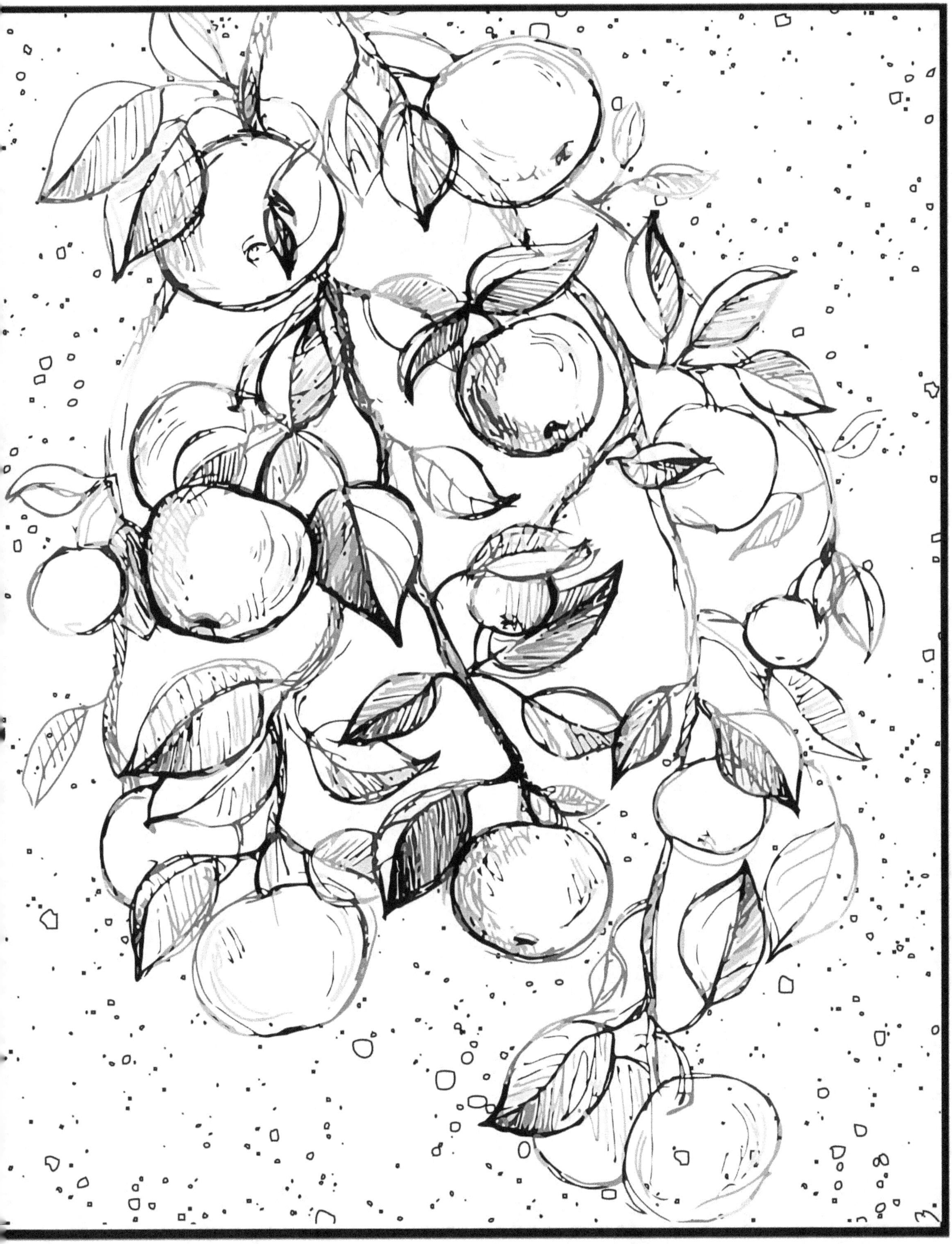

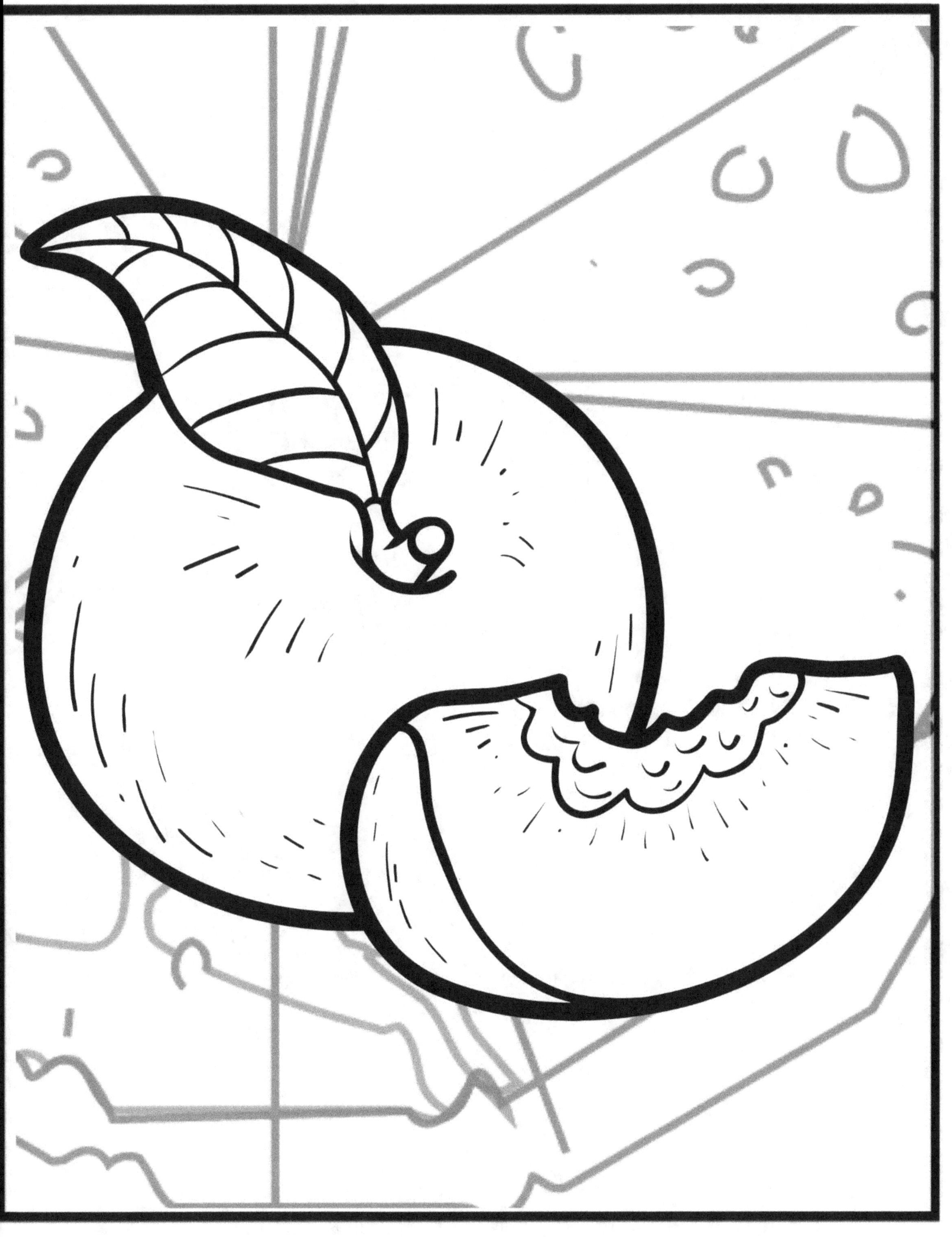

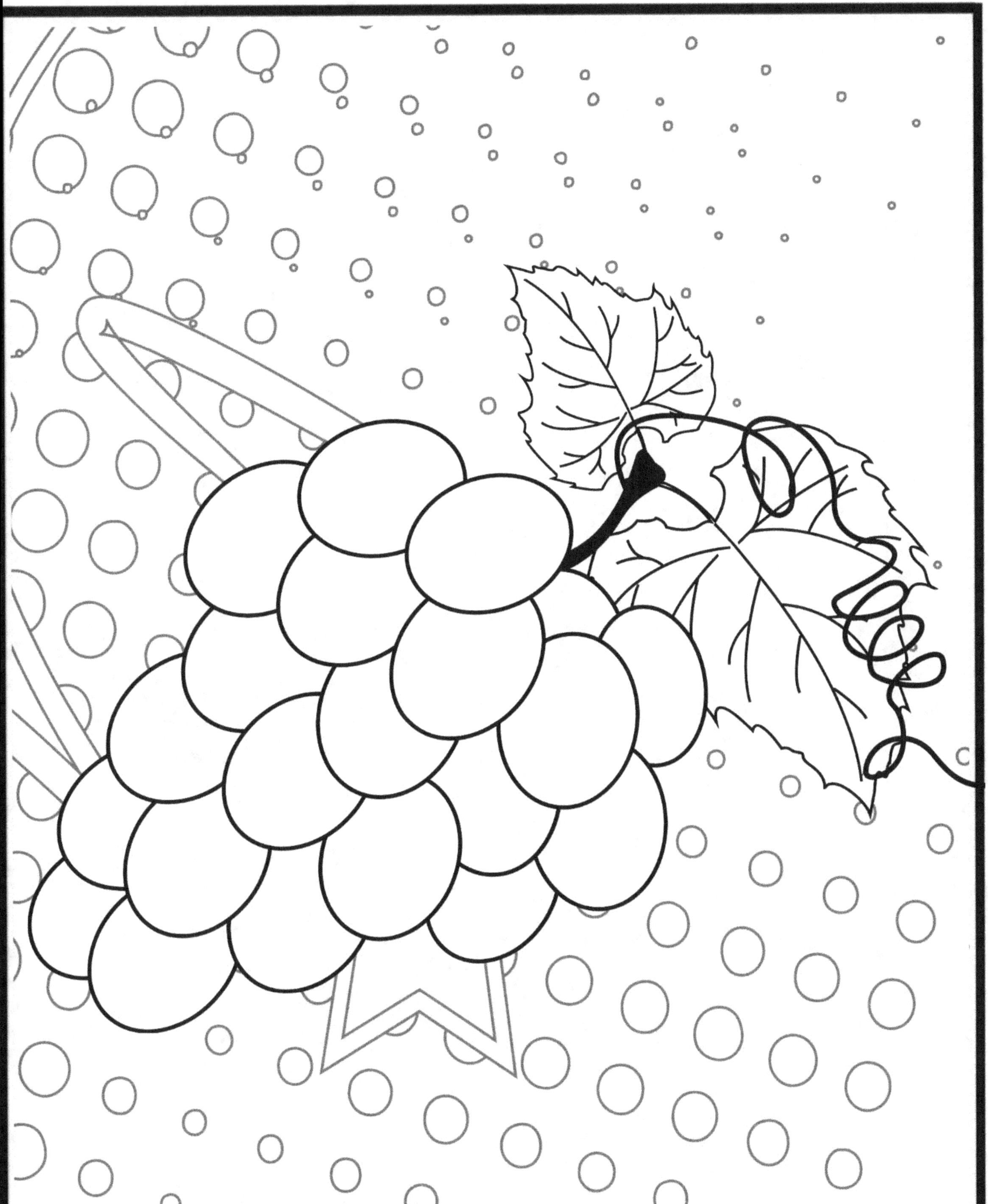

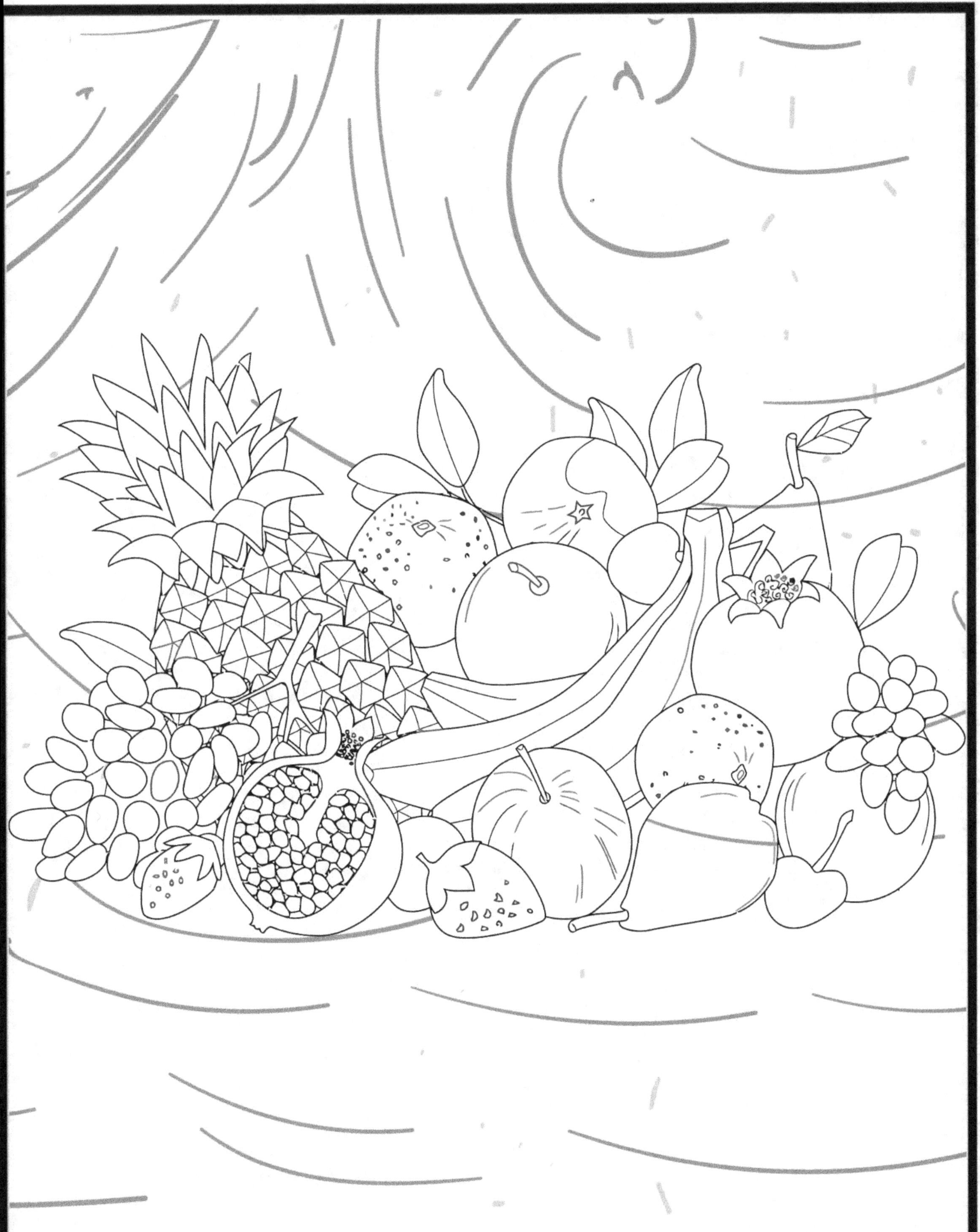

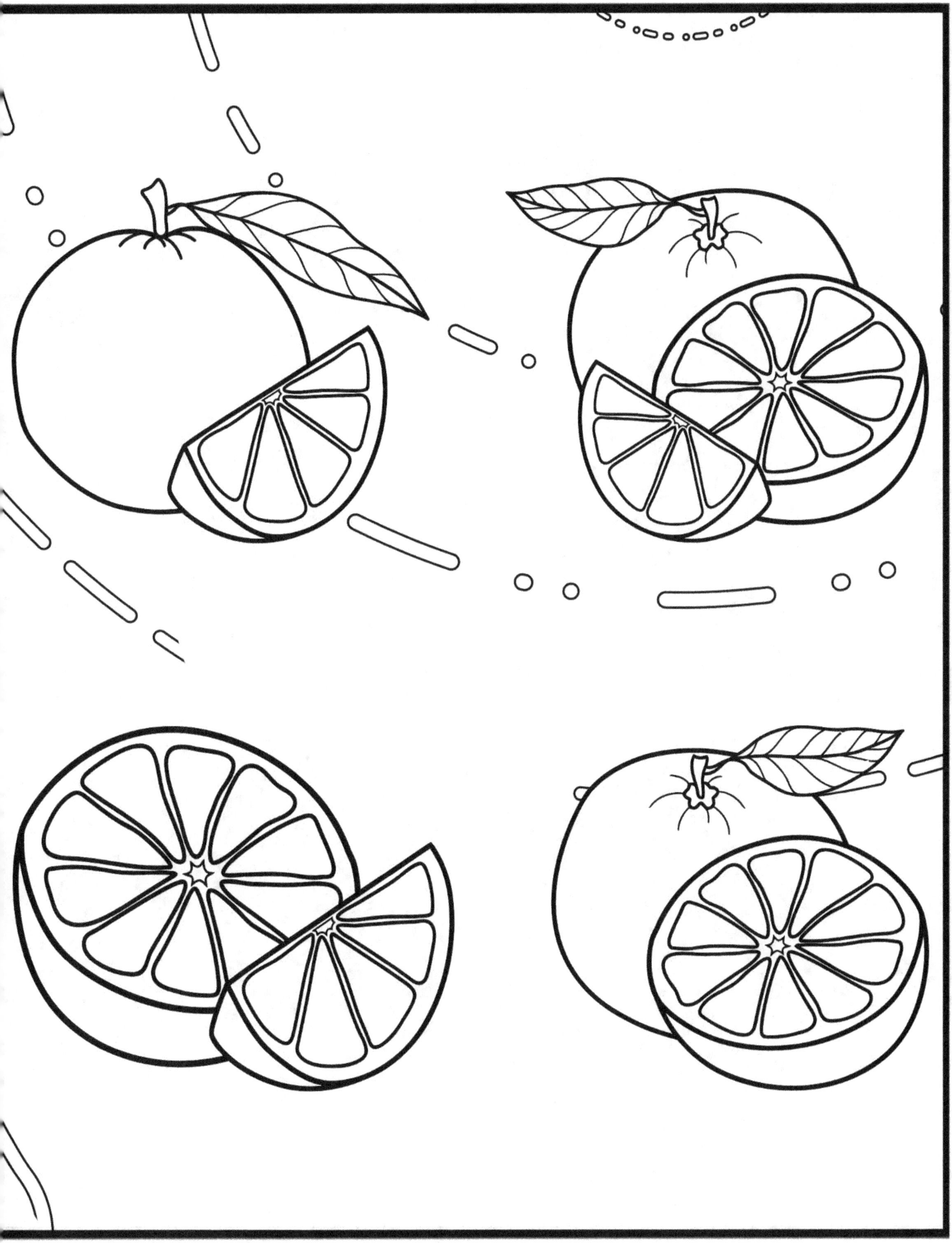

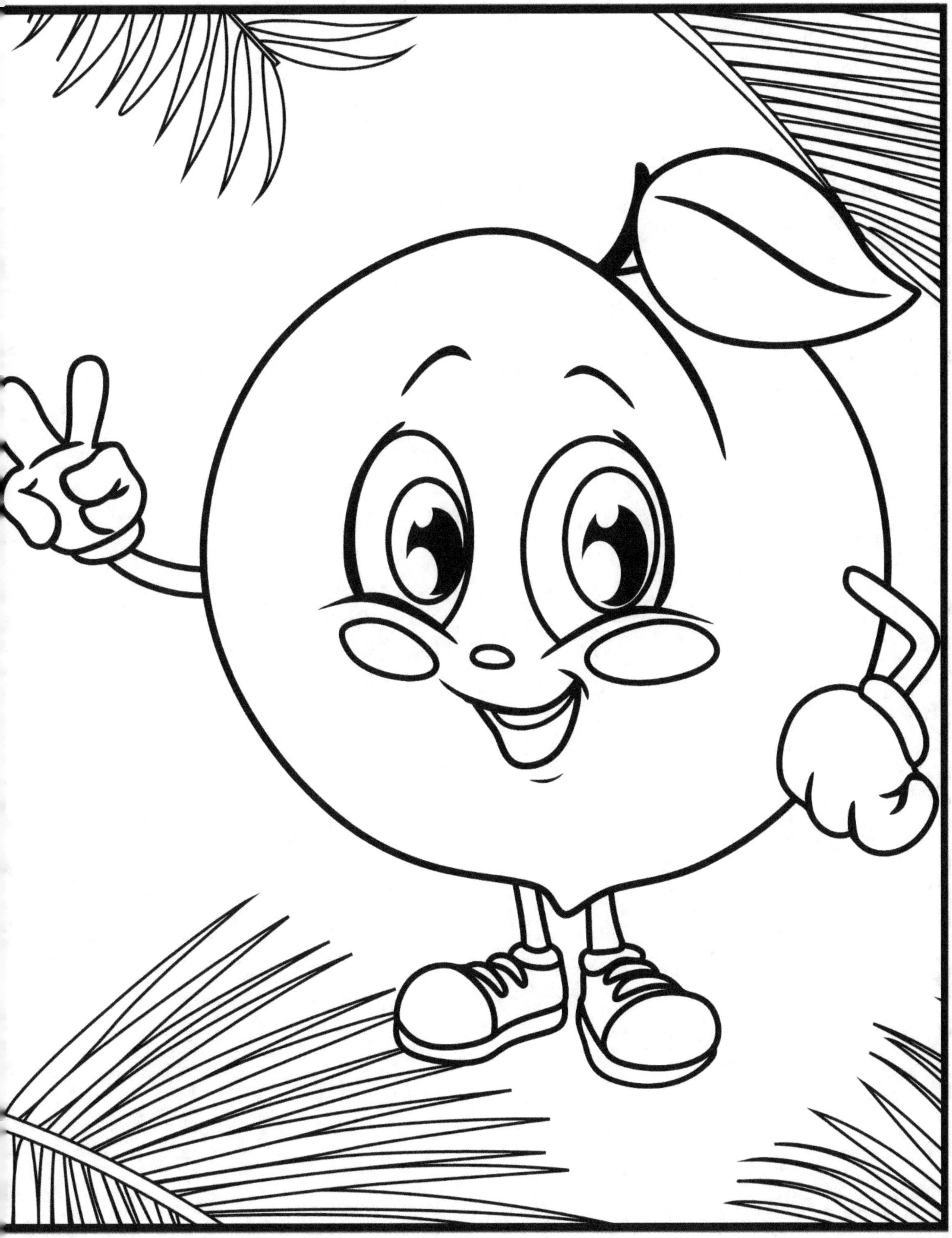

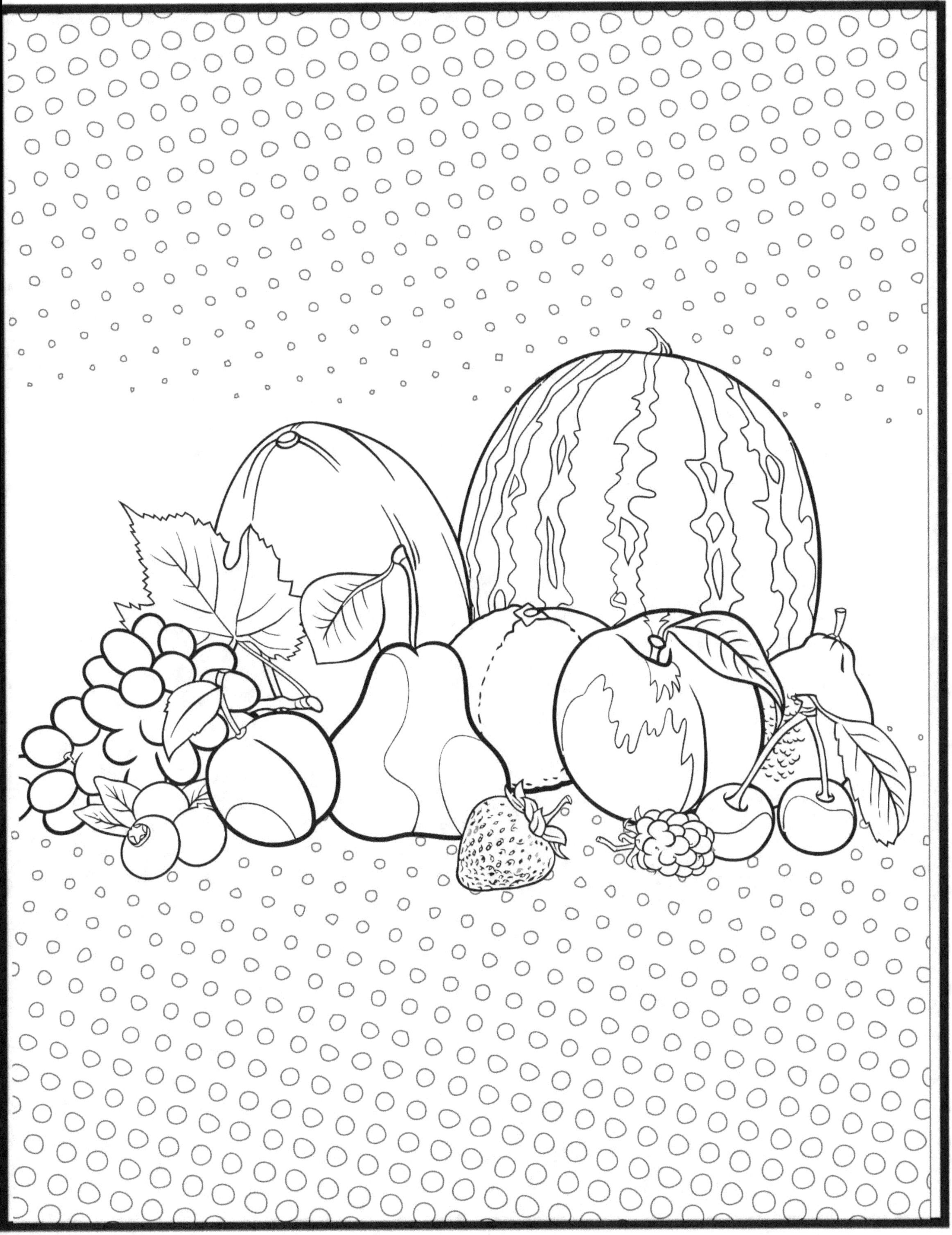

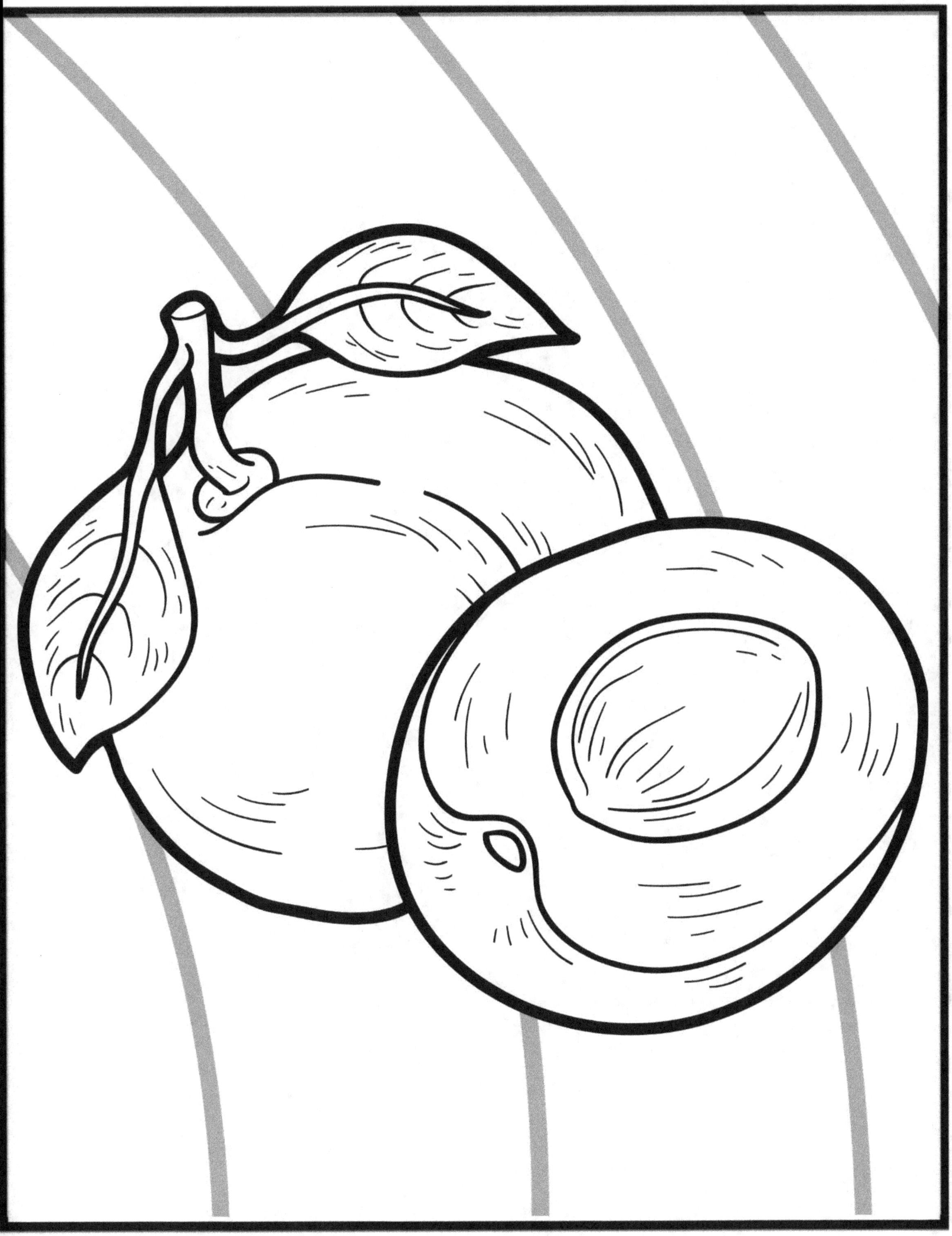

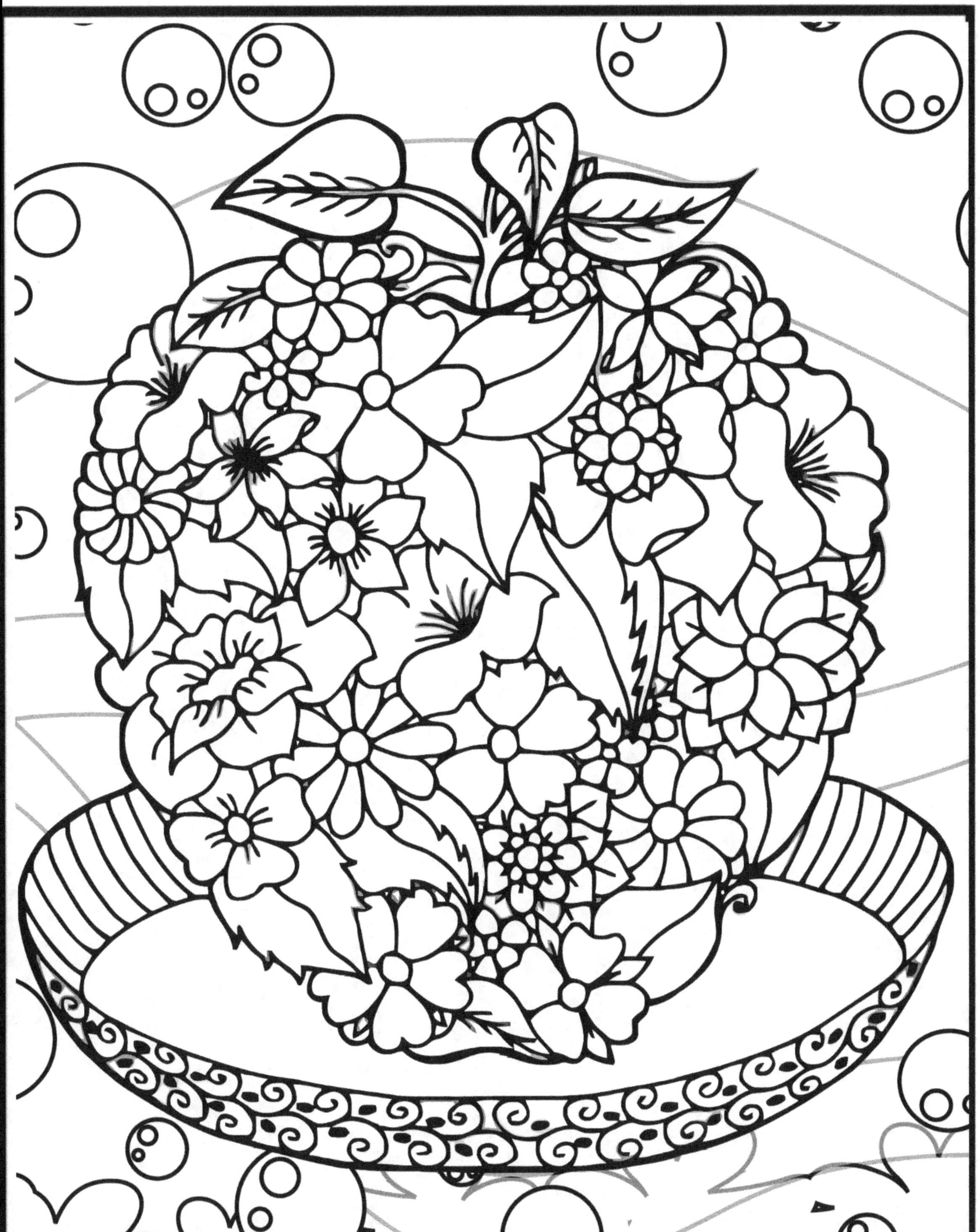

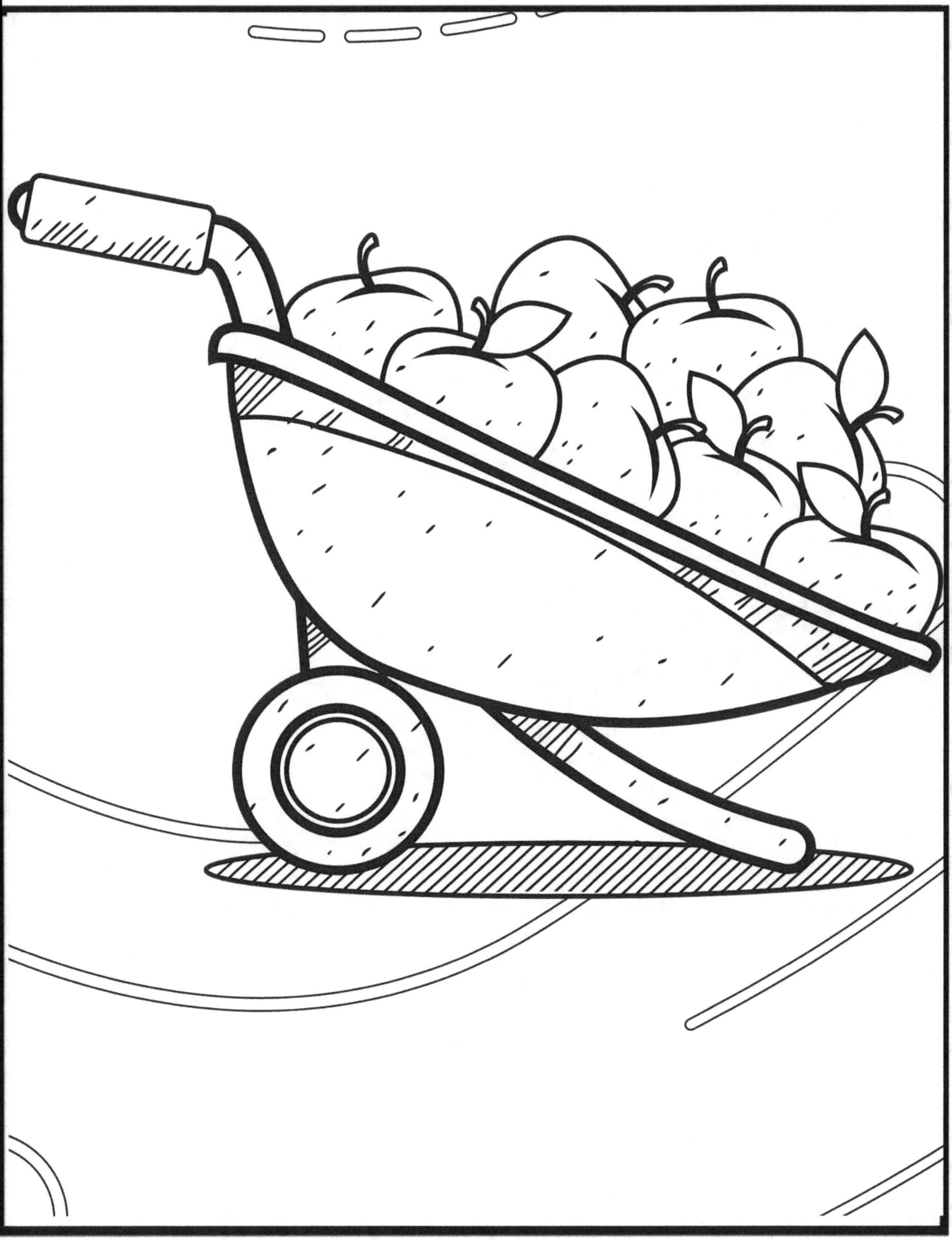

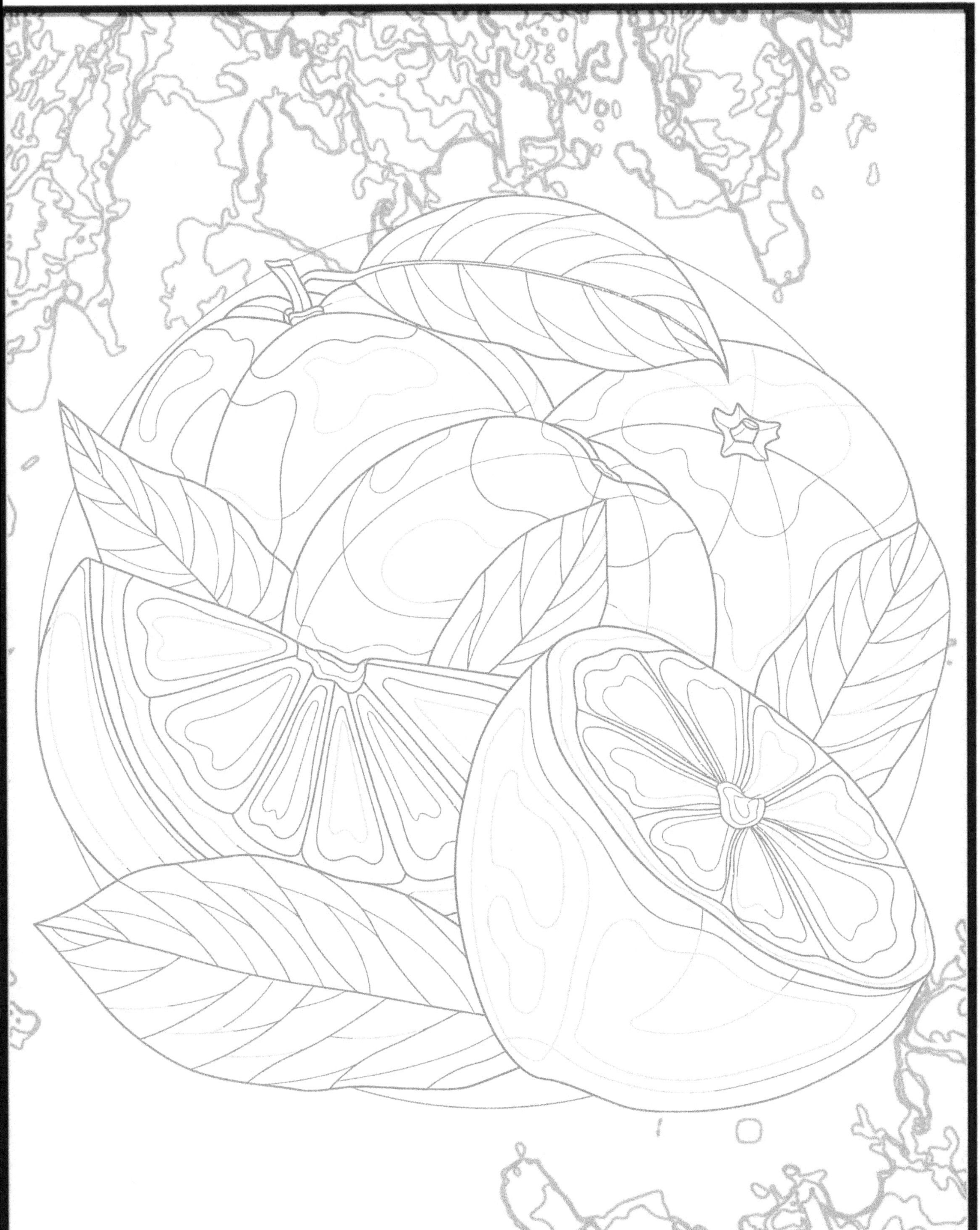

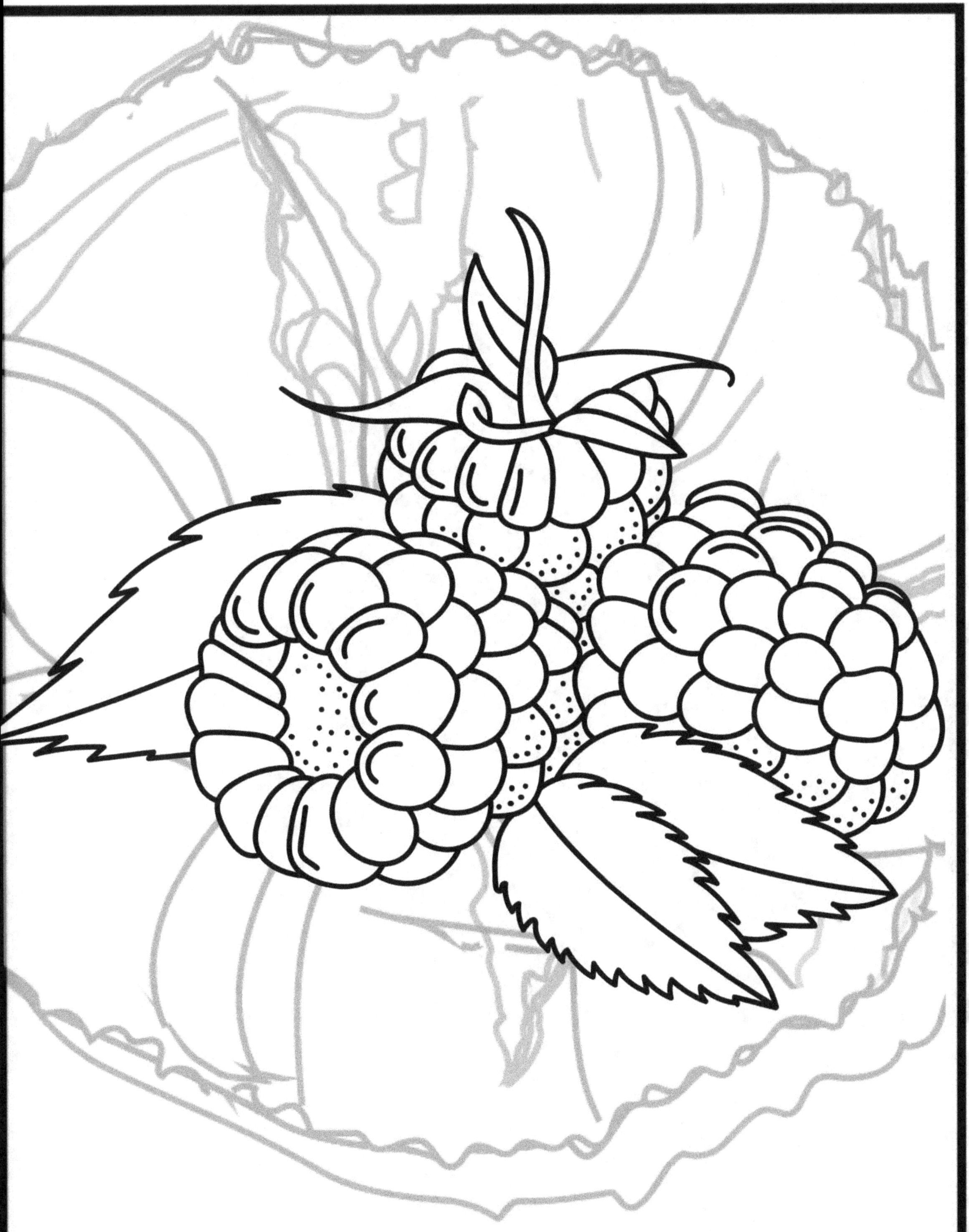

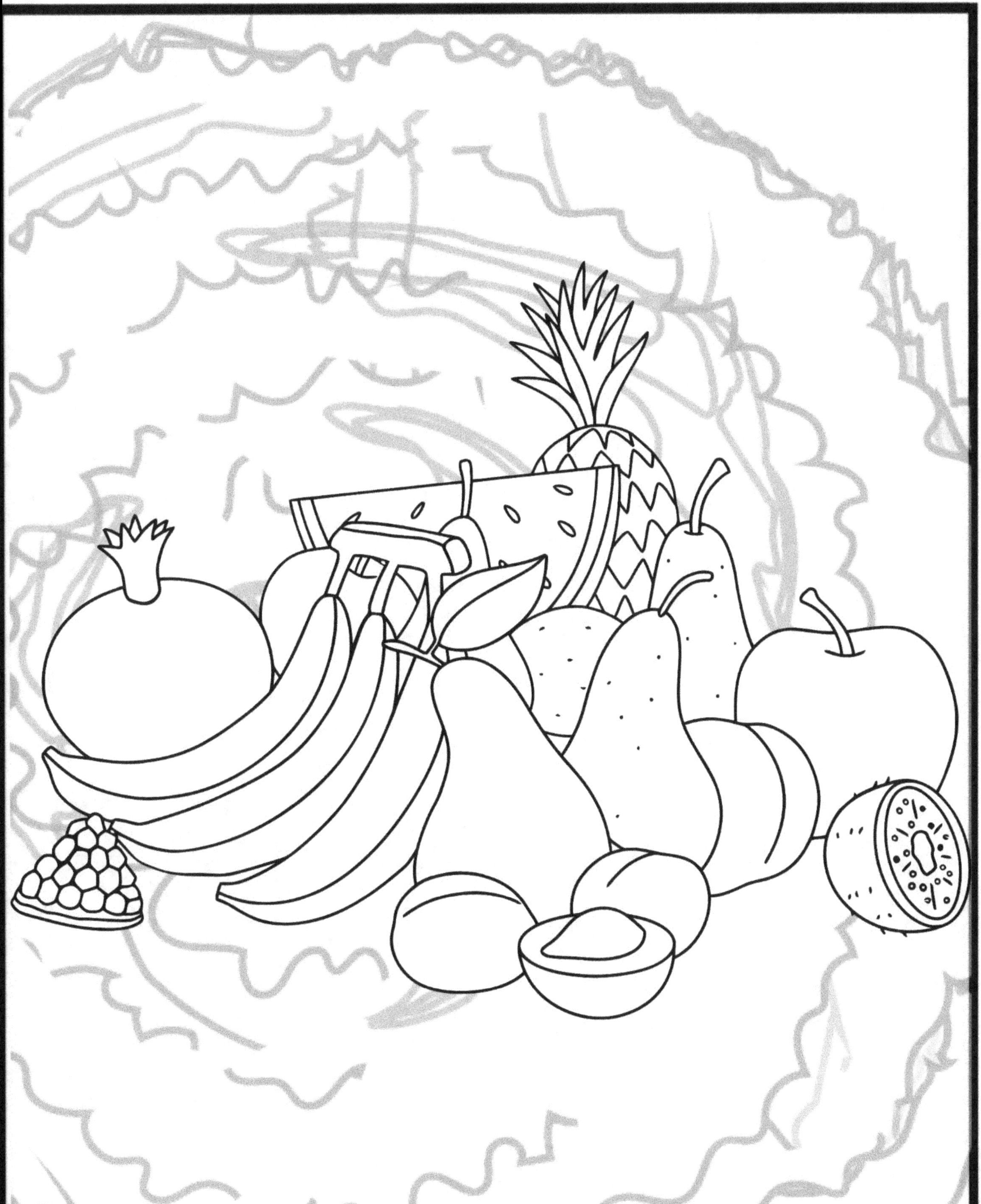

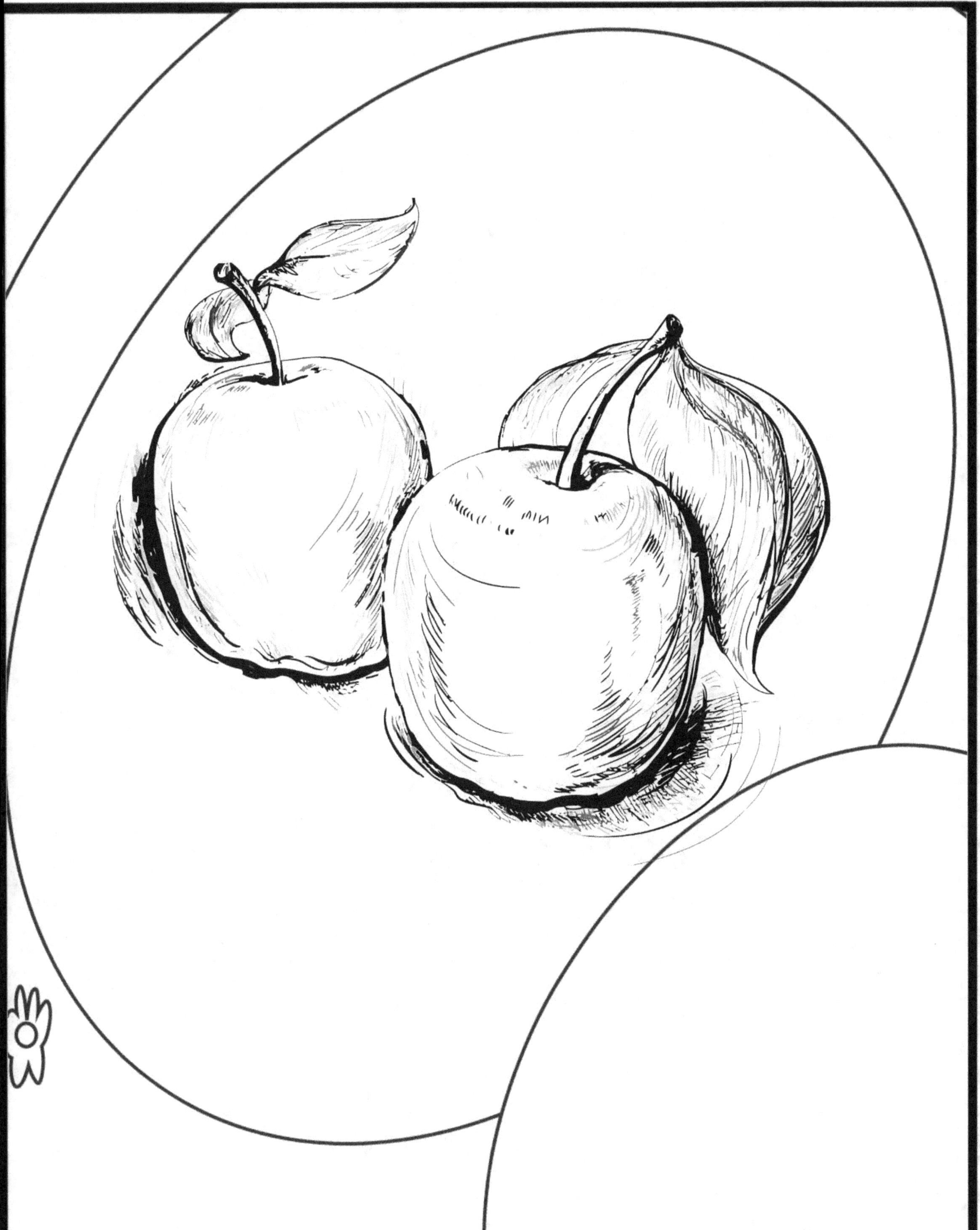

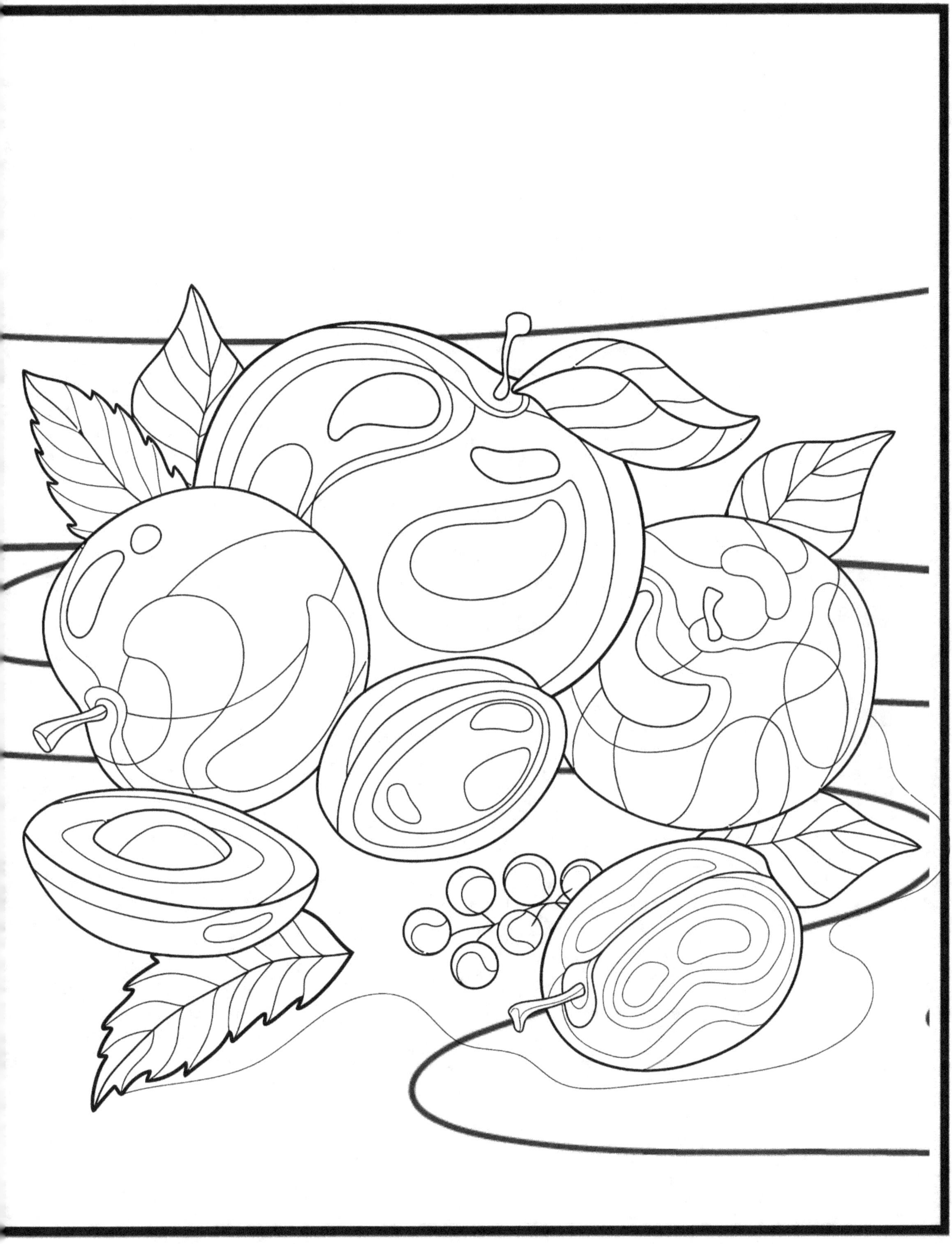

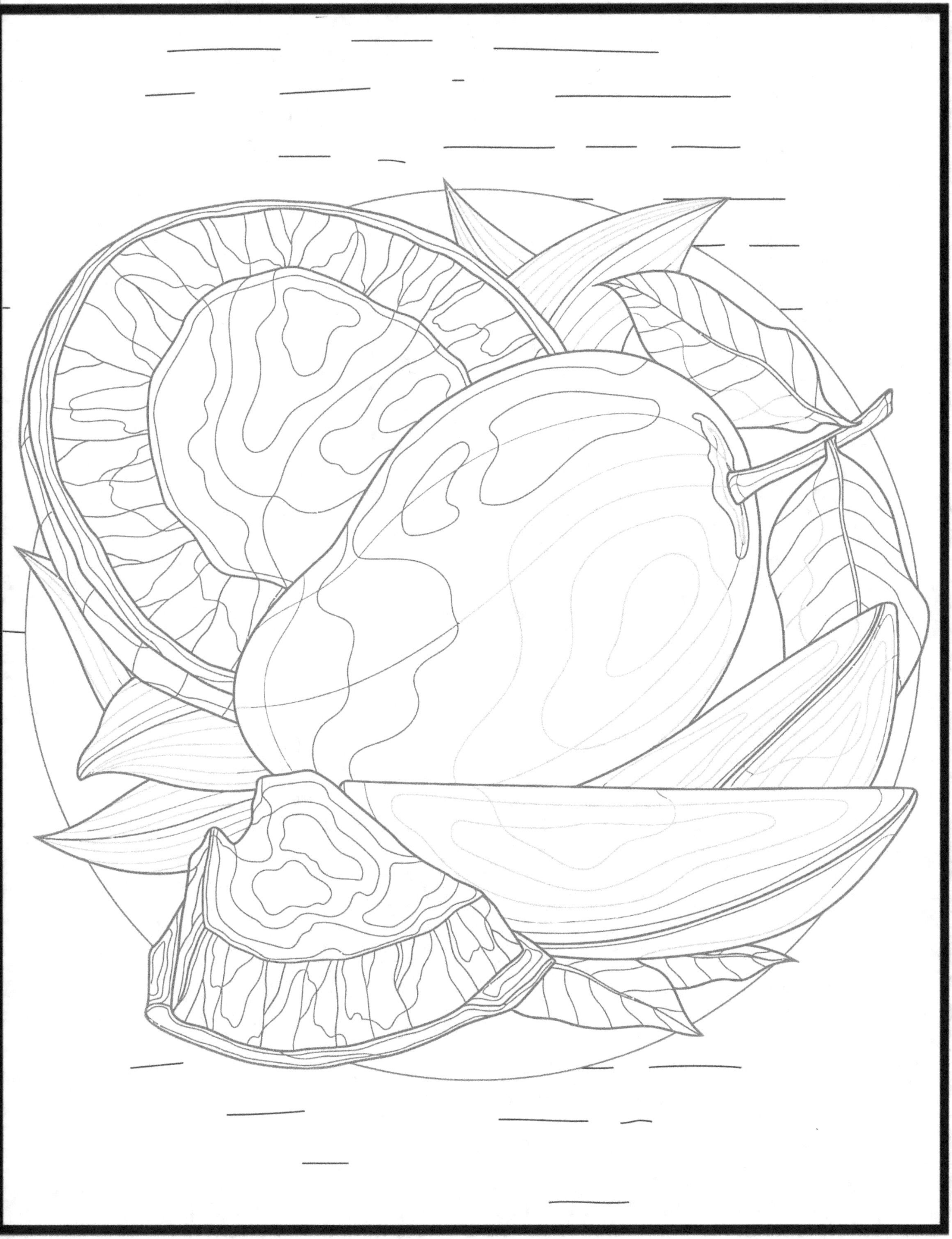

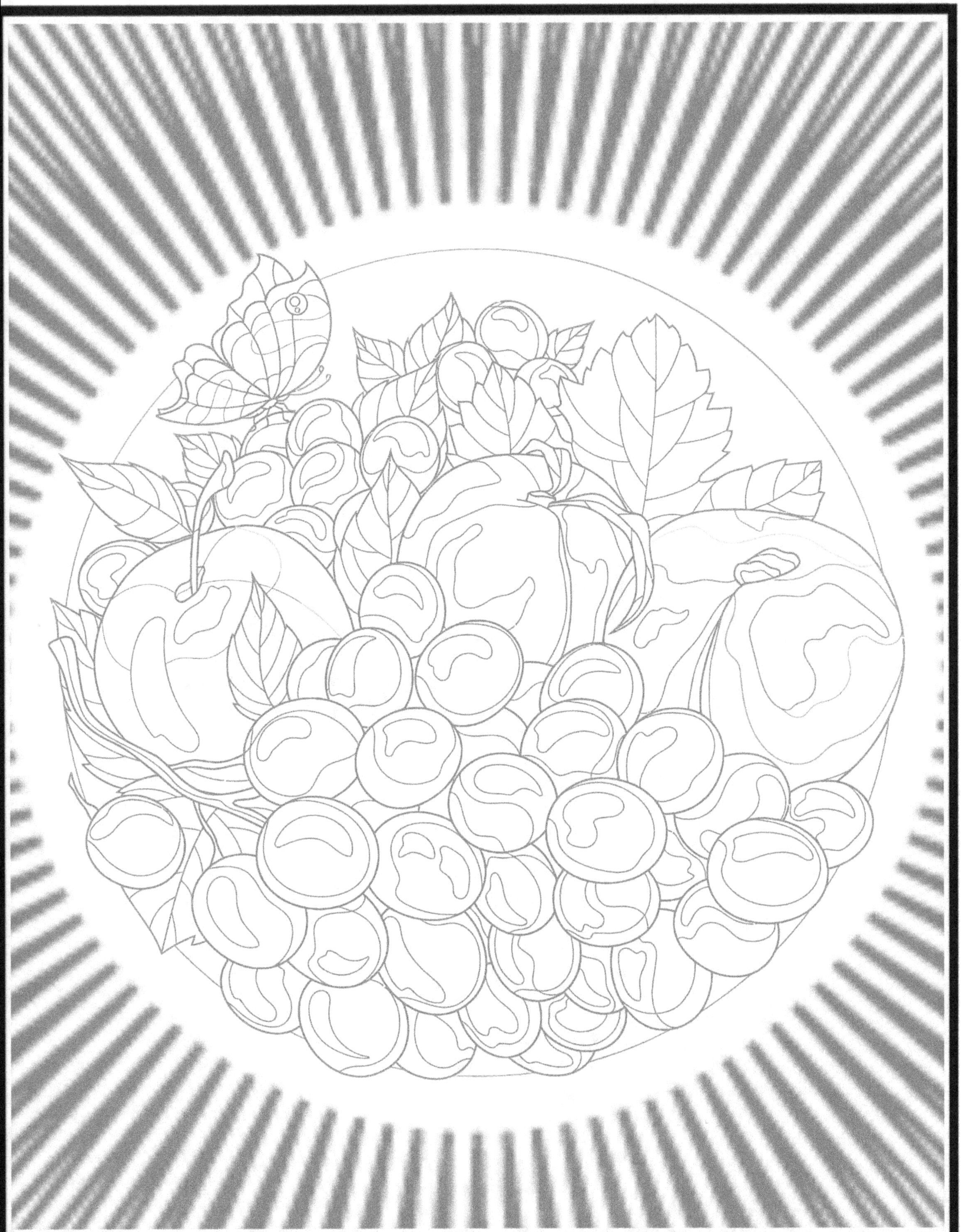

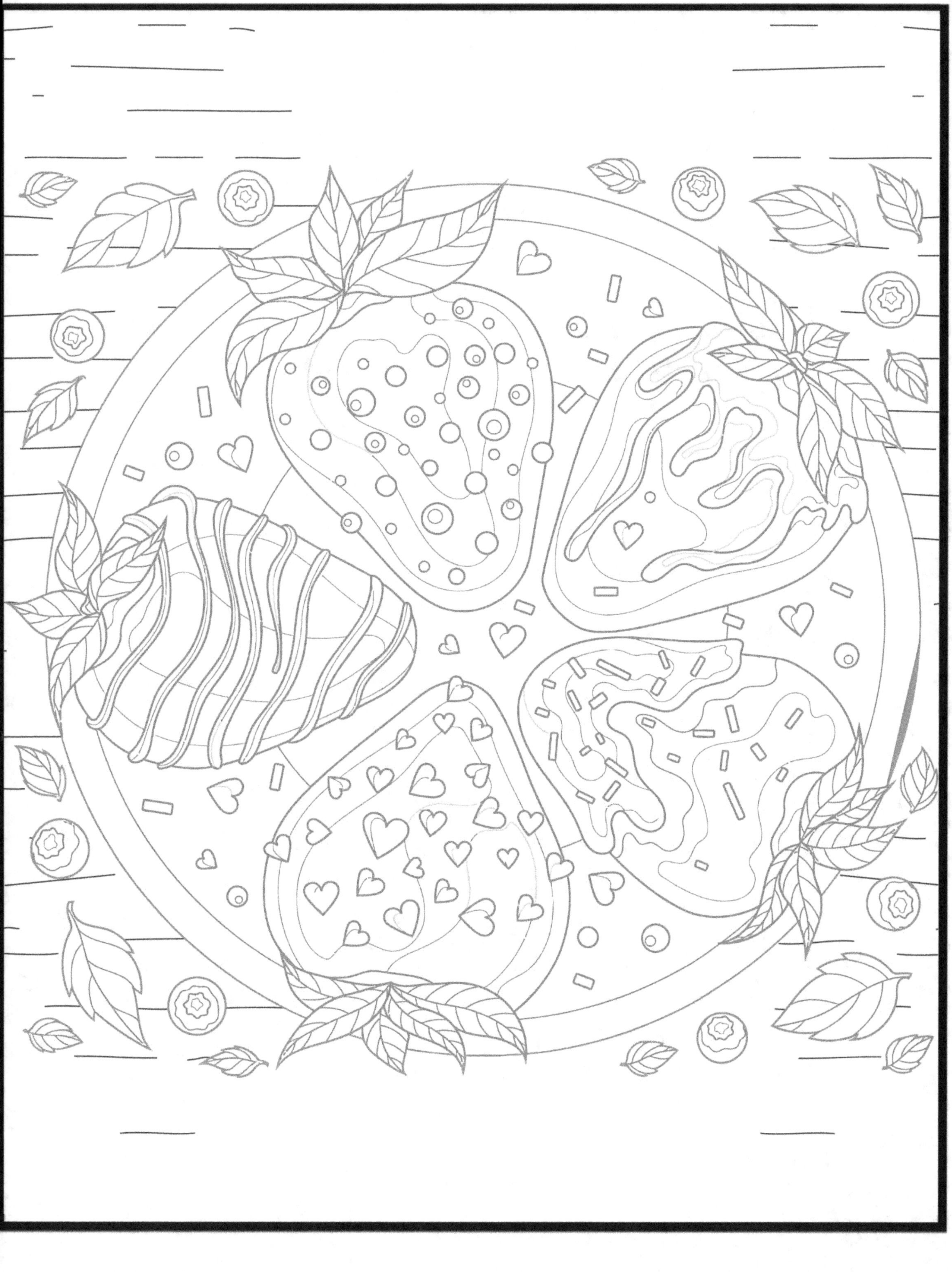

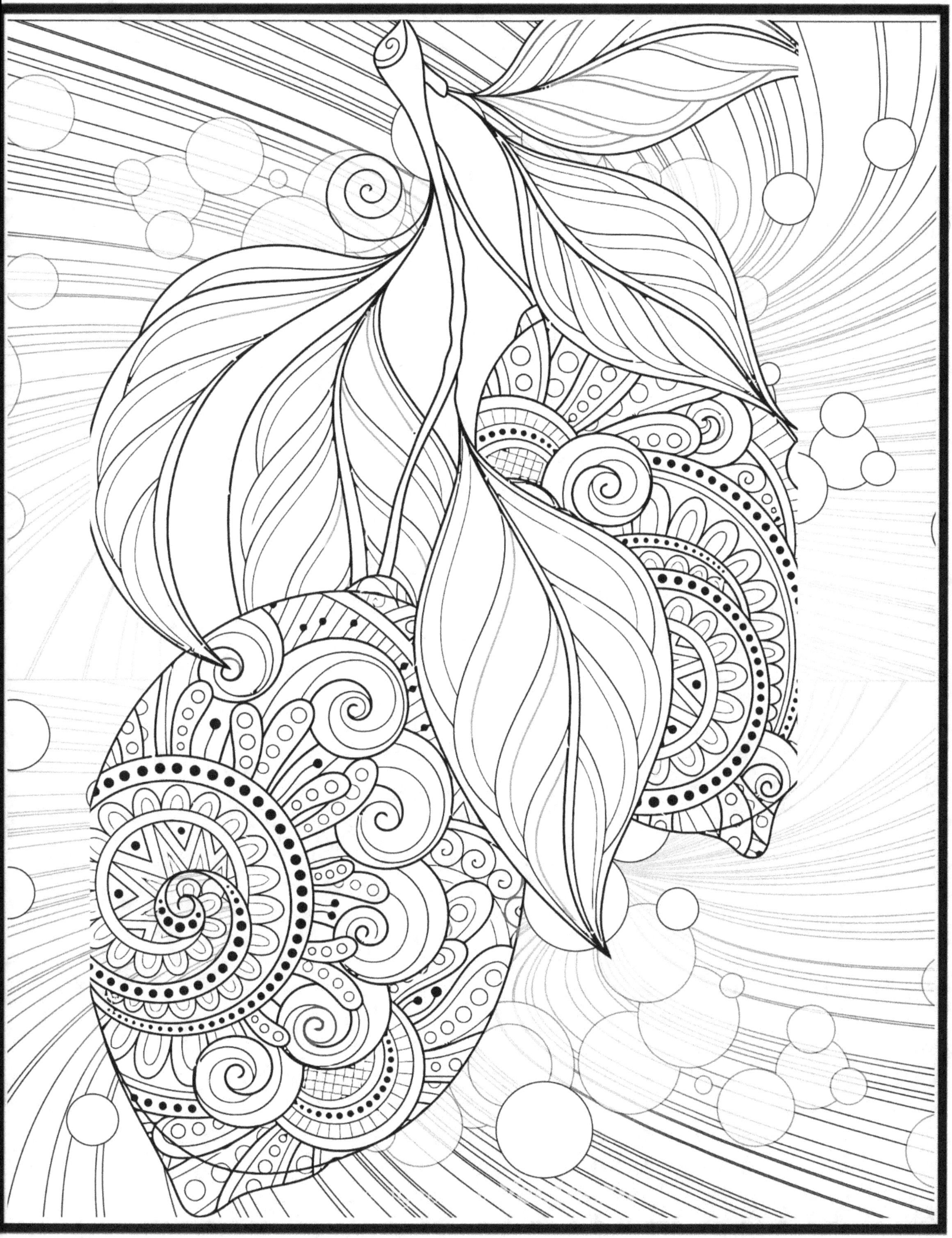

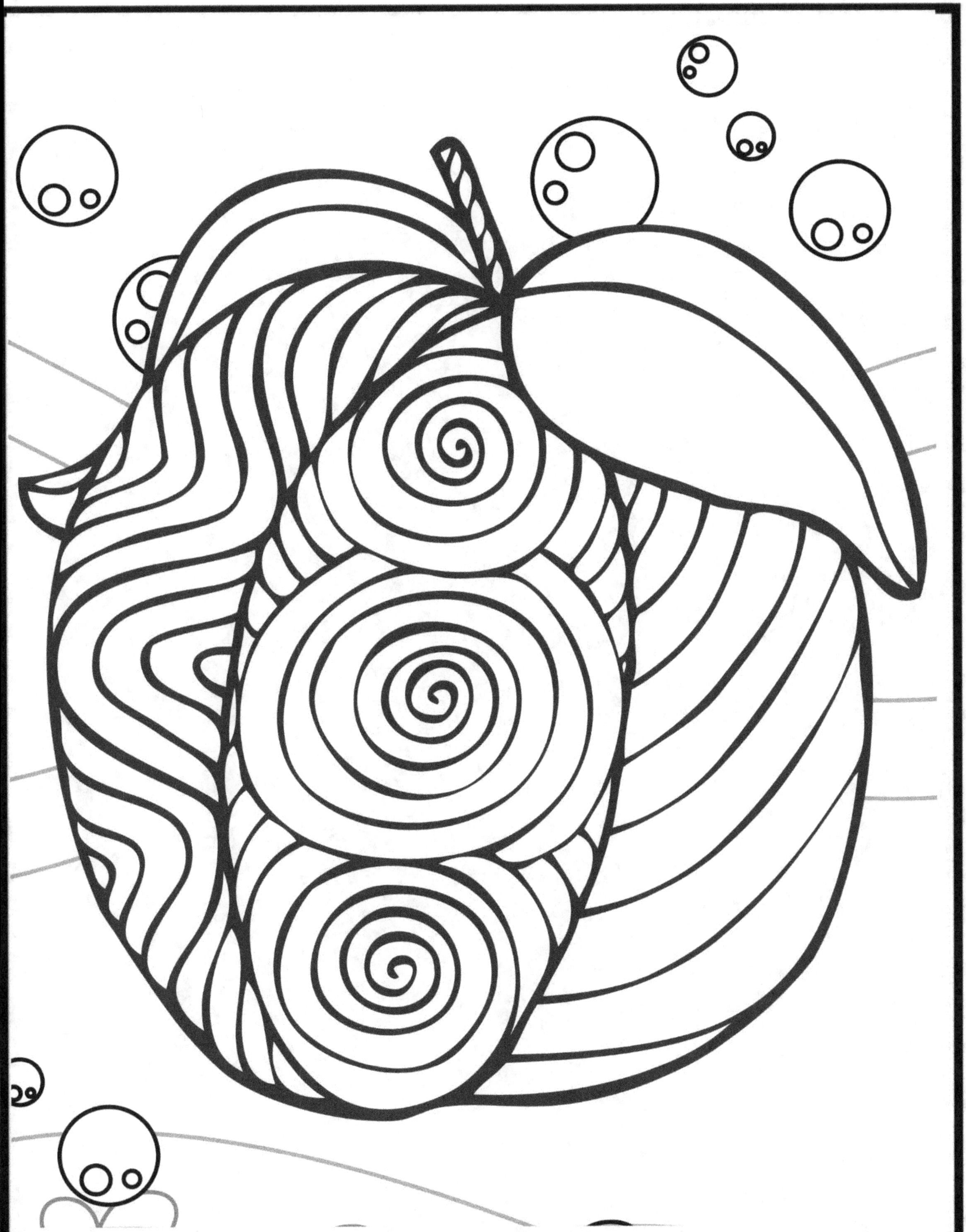

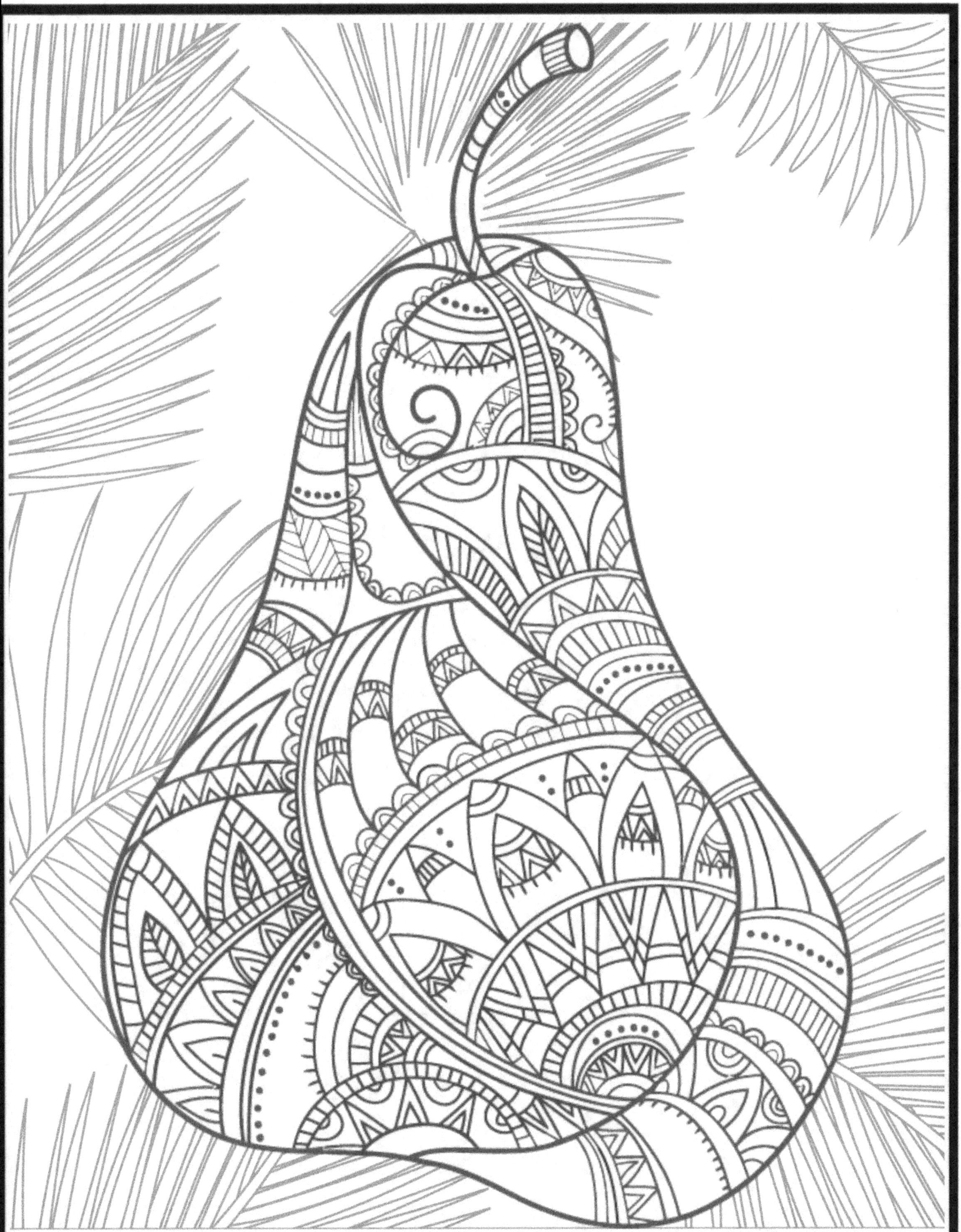

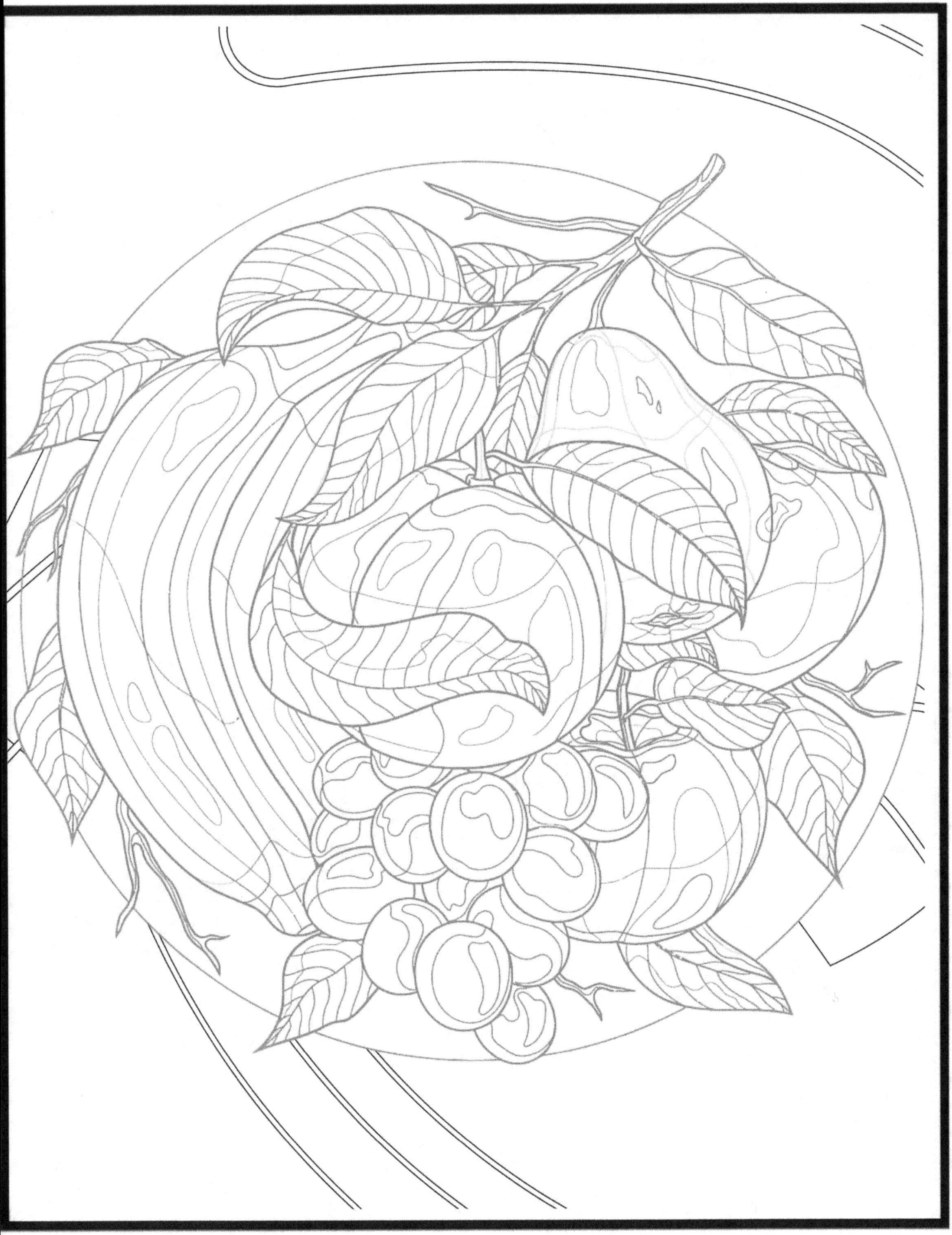

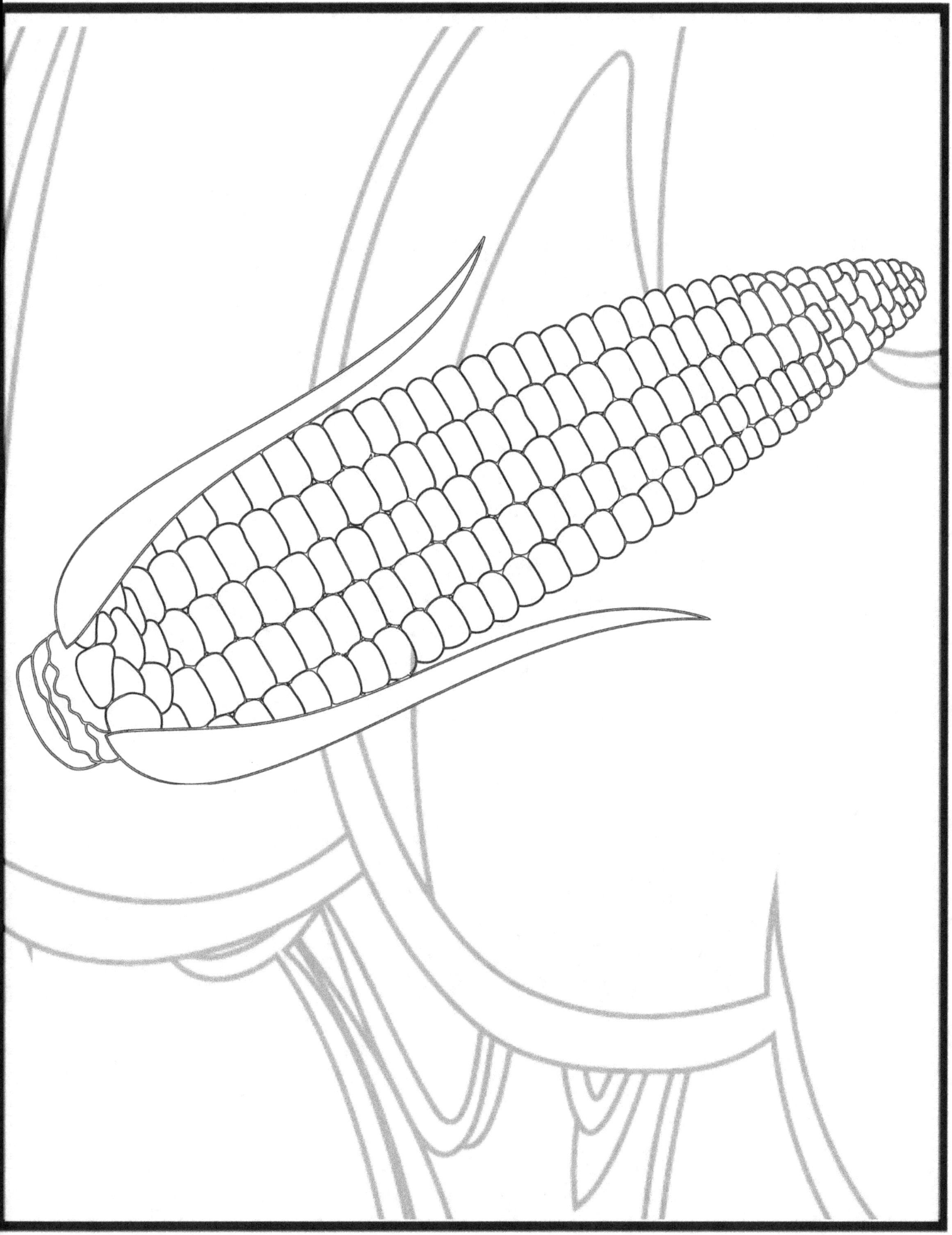

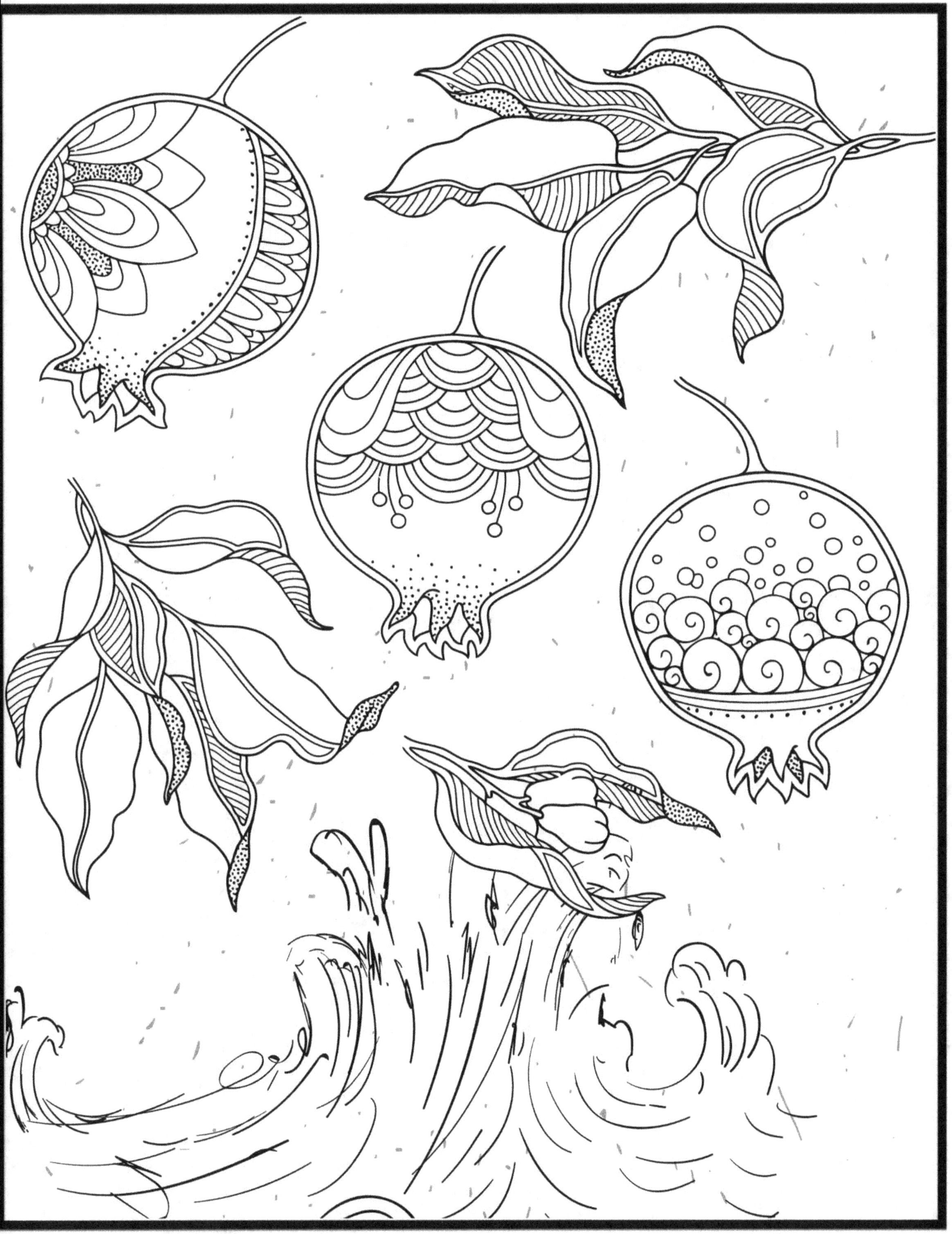

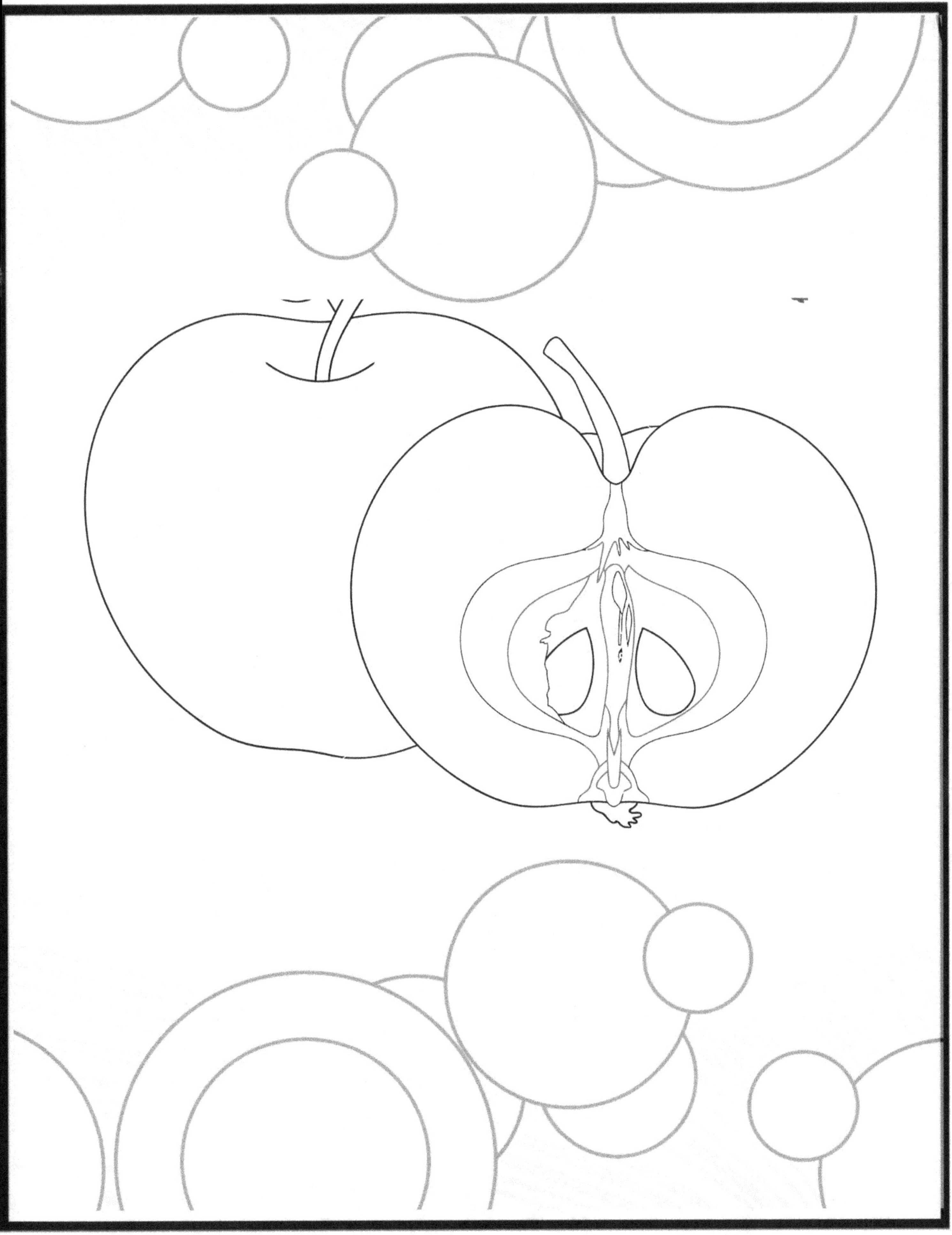

www.ingramcontent.com/pod-product-compliance
Lightning Source LLC
Chambersburg PA
CBHW080522220526
45465CB00006B/2567
9798749754087